# Remember Every Name Every Time

**Corporate America's Memory Master
Reveals His Secrets**

## Benjamin Levy

A FIRESIDE BOOK *Published by Simon & Schuster*
New York London Toronto Sydney Singapore

To my wife, Jenifer,

and my sons, Nathaniel and Declan,

who make every day bright

and unforgettable

FIRESIDE
Rockefeller Center
1230 Avenue of the Americas
New York, NY 10020

For information regarding special discounts for bulk purchases,
please contact Simon & Schuster Special Sales at 1-800-456-6798
or business@simonandschuster.com

Photographs in chapters 2, 4, 11, copyright 2001, Shonna Valeska.
Memory Expert from "The Bob and Ray Radio Show" (Bob Elliott and Ray Goulding).
Used with permission.
Executives quoted in this book are identified by their title at the time they were interviewed.

Designed by Bonni Leon-Berman

Manufactured in the United States of America

1   3   5   7   9   10   8   6   4   2

Library of Congress Cataloging-in-Publication Data is available.

ISBN 0-684-87393-1

**CONTENTS**

kids' names and maybe even the last topic you two discussed. Here's how to remember it *all*.

Ideally, you'll always be on your game, with the FACE and NAME techniques operating like well-oiled machinery. But someone, somewhere, is going to catch you off guard. Here's how to cope when your mind goes blank.

You only need to remember some names for an hour or two. Others for a week. Then there are the ones you know you'll need for years. I've saved the best for last. Maybe you've met one of my CEO clients who's impressed you. His secret? Read on. . . .

Now you've got all my trade secrets for remembering names and faces. Certainly, these skills can have the same beneficial effects on your career that they've had on mine!

I've done the research for you: I studied the most popular names in past decades and compiled a list of the 40 men's and 40 women's names you're most likely to encounter in the business world today. Plus: how to adapt the names for use with the FACE and NAME techniques.

# Everyone Wants a Great Memory. Guess What? You *Already* Have One . . .

Read this brief chapter now, before you leave the bookstore. You'll discover that you already possess tremendous untapped memory-power.

"People are always saying to me, 'I can't believe you remember my name!' I think that remembering names is the heart of good business. It creates a positive environment in the office that helps retain employees, and it's very effective, in a business relationship, in getting the other person to have a good feeling about you."

—*Thomas C. Quick, President, Quick & Reilly/Fleet Securities, Inc.*

I bet you're one of those people who say, "I've got a terrible memory for names." I know that, because it's one of the most common complaints you'll hear—even from highly intelligent and successful people, in all walks of life. Throughout this book, you'll hear "I just can't remember names" from giants of business and industry as well as those on the first rung of success. In my career, I've been fortunate to work with some of the world's most successful people. I've heard it over and over again.

But I'd like to let you in on a little secret. . . .

*They're wrong.*

Why? Because *anyone, and I mean anyone, can develop their memory's natural power* with a little help—the help you'll find in this book.

You probably wouldn't be reading this unless you thought that you could use help in that department. And yet, have you ever considered *how* to improve your memory for names and faces? Have you tried to learn a technique that would *help* you remember them? Probably not—no doubt because you're convinced that your memory for names and faces is "terrible." I hear that lament all the time and, frankly, it drives me crazy, because I know that most people's memory is simply untrained. I also know that *you already possess an innate ability to remember much more than you ever suspected.*

People who've never had a skiing lesson in their lives don't automatically say, "I'm a terrible skier." No—they say, "I don't know how to ski." Some people may be natural skiers, who just clamp on a pair of Rossignols for the first time and fly down the mountain. At the other end of the spectrum are people like me—those who break a leg just by looking up at a chair lift. In between these two types are the vast majority of people, who can benefit enormously from lessons with a ski instructor. Well, I'm here to be your mental ski instructor. (Who knows? Maybe you're a natural who just needs to be pointed in the right direction!) I'll show you the techniques I've developed over the past two decades as a corporate entertainer. Techniques that enable me—night after night after night—to remember the names of more than 100 guests at business get-togethers, all of them *people I've just met!*

# Starting Right Now,
# Unlock Your Memory Power!

The most effective tool for memorization is the brain's ability to form *visual images.* Seeing something in your mind—reading a description, then looking away and revisualizing it—is more effective than simply plowing through written text. As an example, I'm going to tell you a surreal little story that—although admittedly wacky—will nonetheless give you an amazing insight into how memory works. It won't take long, just a couple of minutes at most. At the end, I promise that you will be rewarded with concrete, indisputable evidence that your memory is more powerful than you ever imagined.

# Here's the Key

*See the story.* Don't just *skim.* Don't even just *read* the story. Truly *visualize* it. If I mention a fire, try to see the fire in as much detail as possible. Is it orange at the top and blue at the bottom, or the other way around? Are sparks flying? Does the smoke smell wonderful, like a roaring fireplace on a cold winter day, or does it burn your eyes and lungs? If you concentrate on the story, visualizing each image in vivid detail, you'll get a firsthand demonstration of the memory power you already possess—power that *Remember Every Name Every Time* will show you how to harness and use in running your company or building your career. This power will even help you sail through the kinds of social situations which in the past have left you feeling mortified about forgetting someone's name.

Okay, here's the story. Start reading. And remember:

### VISUALIZE!

You're in your office when the acrid smell of burning tar begins to fill the room. You start to go out into the hall to investigate but stop short when you see the office door. The door has a big letter X ON it, sloppily painted in tar so hot that the X ON the door is still smoking and sizzling. You rush into the hallway to see who's responsible for this vandalism and are stunned: the hallway had only recently been painted a lemony yellow, but now its pristine surfaces have been wrecked, every WALL MARRED by a series of these foul-smelling, smoky X's. You follow the trail, the pungent odor becoming stronger as you get closer to the source of one WALL MARR after another. Then you turn the corner and your jaw drops in astonishment: GENERAL Douglas MacArthur is standing there, complete with corncob pipe and aviator sunglasses, holding a bucket of tar and a sticky paintbrush in his blackened hands. GENERAL MacArthur is so startled at being caught that the pipe drops out of his mouth, falling with a hiss into the bucket of tar.

*Take a break right here and try to recall what you've just read. Look away from the book for a moment. Think about what has happened in this story so far.*

You're back? Did you think about the story? Did it all begin in a generic office building? Did someone imitating Zorro scratch the letter Z on a window? Was General Colin Powell the culprit? No, it all started in *your* office, and it was the letter X on your *door* and in a *hallway*, painted in tar by General *MacArthur*, right? This information would be almost impossible to get wrong if you truly visualized it: the smoke curling up from the tar; the walls' fresh coat of yellow paint; the gleam of MacArthur's aviator sunglasses. Every detail, brought into sharper focus *by your own imagination*, etches the story into your memory. Okay, let's get back to it and . . .

## VISUALIZE, VISUALIZE, VISUALIZE!

MacArthur drops the bucket and brush and runs down the hall and out of the building to his car, a perfectly restored red FORD Model T. MacArthur gives the old-fashioned hand crank a turn and the FORD sputters to life. He jumps into the driver's seat and roars away in a choking cloud of exhaust. At the first intersection, MacArthur jams on the brakes, because looming ahead of the GENERAL, in place of a traffic light, is an ELECTRIC chandelier—with red, yellow, and green lightbulbs—that is made to look like MacArthur himself. The GENERAL-shaped ELECTRIC chandelier is hanging so low that the car smashes into it, sending a spray of glittering red, yellow, and green glass shards into the air. As MacArthur speeds away from the collision, he spies you in the rearview mirror and bellows from the open car, "I shall return!"

*That's the end of the story. Run through it again in your mind, re-calling in as much detail as possible the little adventure that begins with the mysterious appearance of a hot-tar X ON your office door, followed by similar WALL MARS; the discovery of GENERAL MacArthur as the perpetrator of the door and wall vandalism; MacArthur's escape in a FORD Model T; and the car's spectacular run-in with a low-slung chandelier that depicts the GENERAL in ELECTRIC red, yellow, and green lights. By concentrating on these details, you'll still have a vivid memory of the story if MacArthur ever makes good on his promise to return.*

# What Was *That* All About?

Now here's the surprise I promised: Without even realizing it, you've just memorized the top five companies of the Fortune 500. That's right. Here they are:

1 Exxon—your hint in the story is the **X ON** the door and in the hall
2 Wal-Mart—the **WALL MARS** of hot tar makes this memory stick
3 General Motors—signified by **GENERAL** MacArthur
4 Ford Motor Company—MacArthur flees in a **FORD** Model T
5 General Electric—as revealed in the smashing tribute to the **GENERAL** with **ELECTRIC** lighting

# A Little Trick
# with Big Implications

Skeptics might pooh-pooh this exercise, saying that most people could remember a list of five names without visualizing anything. Agreed. But they'd certainly struggle to remember the list days or weeks later. They also might have trouble remembering them in correct order right from the start. Was that General Electric or General Motors that was number three? Following the line of the story, you'd never mix them up.

*But there's much more at work here than just remembering the Fortune 500's top five.*

On the simple matter of remembering the names of companies, the story could go on and on, with one event leading to another in its improbable and cartoonish way, until you've committed to memory the top 25 or 50 or 100 companies in the Fortune 500.

*Once the narrative sequence begins, it can be extended to embody almost any list you want to memorize.*

How to memorize lists is not what this prologue is about, though. I just used this example to help you glimpse the power of your own mind, your ability to enhance your memory through concentration, visualization and imagination. Even in our two-minute drill, you put those skills to work in a concerted way that provided a tangible memory reward. The story needed to be strange, even startling, because a string of unremarkable details wouldn't have captured your attention. The generic and bland is forgettable. The peculiar and amusing is not.

Over breakfast tomorrow, imagine the smell of burning tar that begins the tale, and you'll be delighted to find that you remember not only the whole story of General MacArthur's alarming visit, but also the Fortune 500 top five. Again, that's a very modest sample of how your memory power can be trained. By the end of this book, you'll be ready to tackle all five hundred.

# You've Unlocked the Door. Now Step Inside with Me.

Even before learning about me and my techniques for radically improving your ability to remember names and faces, you've gotten a glimpse of the **untapped memory power you already possess.** Believe me: you *don't* have "a terrible memory for names." You've got a *terrific* memory for names; you just need to find it, train it and put it into action. That will happen for you with the help of this book.

# Introduction

"When you perform for us, Benjamin, a variety of clients and bank people coming from different places all share in the wonders of your performance. Everyone is amazed at the experience. But when you connect everyone name by name and have them all gasping, the crowd becomes one homogeneous group. In situations where we're trying to meet clients and connect quickly, that's enormously positive."

—*Douglas A. Warner III, Chairman and CEO, J.P. Morgan Chase*

Perhaps you've also heard of Edgar Bronfman Jr., of Seagram fame? Or Art Ryan, chairman and CEO of Prudential Financial? Or Henry Kravis, co-founder of Kohlberg Kravis Roberts & Co.? Or Bill Esrey, Sprint chairman and CEO?

These are some of the most successful individuals in corporate America. They're also my clients. As an entertainer who works solely for the most senior executives of the world's top-rated multinational companies, I perform at exclusive private parties and major company functions that are hosted by these and many other renowned business legends.

Here's a brief idea of what I do: During a dinner for, say, 100 to 150 people, I go from table to table meeting each guest. I entertain briefly at every table with some sleight-of-hand. For example, I take blank pieces of paper from my wallet that magically become hundred-dollar bills. Or, with a guest totally unaware of what I'm doing, I remove his watch from his wrist and return it to him before I move on. Most important, while I'm doing this I get the name of each person at the table. Then when dessert is served, I do a show for the whole room, with audience volunteers helping me to pull off effects that are even more surprising and get even bigger laughs.

But no matter how much applause and delighted laughter my

magic gets, by far the biggest reaction is for the last part of my act. That's when I ask everyone to stand up and only sit down again when I have thanked them individually, by name, for coming to my show. As each person sits down, the suspense mounts: can I really remember the name of everyone in the room? People I've *just* met? When I come to the last person and finish without having stumbled over a single name, even the toughest, no-nonsense businessman in the room claps and cheers. A standing ovation, more often than not.

It was a long road to the memory performance I do today from the first basic memory tricks I performed as a young magician in high school and college. Then, armed with a drama degree, the beginnings of a magic act and little else up my sleeve I embarked upon my professional career. My simple memory tricks (which involved more trick than memory) always got a nice round of applause and quickly became an important part of my performances. But soon I became intrigued and motivated to take this "memory business" a step or two further. That decision launched me on a period of study and exploration of the mysteries of memory. I read every book I could find on the subject and through trial, and some embarrassing errors in my early performances, I learned what worked and what didn't. I gradually came to the realization that a good memory or even a great one could be *acquired* by just about anyone. You didn't need a photographic memory or a genius IQ. You just had to educate and discipline your memory. I found this to be particularly true for all those people who were convinced they had a terrible memory for names. So, over the years I developed and refined the memory techniques that are now in this book.

As I used my ability to remember the names of everyone in my audiences, I realized that these highly successful people got a *tremendous* kick out of this seemingly astounding feat. There was something important here. At the risk of sounding immodest, let me share with you what remembering names did for me. Here's William T. Esrey, chairman and CEO of the Sprint Corporation: "Benjamin's memory act is spectacular. His ability to remember the names of everyone in an audience, well over 150 people in each of four performances for Sprint, is unforgettable. His sleight-of-hand magic is equally amazing. But even more extraordinary is his ability to charm and engage everyone in his performance and create the kind of warm, friendly atmosphere we strive for at Sprint Corporation events."

With this kind of reception among executives for my name-remembering demonstrations, I made reeling off their names an even greater part of my show. But it didn't occur to me at first that there was a more important reason, beyond mere entertainment, why a demonstration of a prodigious ability to remember names and faces would strike such a chord with these corporate chieftains.

# A Tutor in the Boardroom

I started to realize there was still another business and personal benefit when a well-known CEO approached me after a performance in the summer of 1994. With a hint of embarrassment, he asked if I would give him a private lesson to help him to remember names better. I thought at first that this executive had enjoyed my performance so much that he wanted to try to wow his friends with his ability to remember names. Sort of the way people ask me to teach them how to do a magic trick (like someone buttonholing a doctor at a party and asking for medical advice). But it quickly became clear that he wasn't interested in entertaining at parties with a memory display. He wanted practical help that would further burnish his already outstanding repertoire of executive skills.

I met with him in his office a few weeks later and taught him the basics of my technique for remembering names. In less than thirty minutes, he was already surprising himself with memory self-tests I had devised the night before by tearing photos of people out of magazines. He seemed very grateful, and I thought that besides helping someone I genuinely liked, it was a good way to make sure his company hired me again the next year.

But then, over the course of the next sixteen months or so, the chairman of a major media company also sought out my tutoring, a Wall Street whiz quietly asked me to give him some tips, and the COO of a telecommunications giant recruited me for an office visit. These weren't just older executives worried about their memories as they aged; a couple of them were in mid-career with not a trace of gray hair, and they, too, were anxious for help remembering names.

I realized that I was tapping into a career skill few people talk about but one that matters vitally even to the most powerful executives in the world. Regardless of how enormous the business successes these men and women had enjoyed, they realized that improving their ability to remember names would give them an edge in taking their careers up another notch. I saw that if these people—all with the proven ability to rise to the top of their profession—recognized the importance of remembering names, then *any* career could benefit. Obviously, salesmen and politicians already knew the value of remembering names and faces. But anyone interested in maximizing their career prospects—lawyers, doctors, teachers, technology developers, entry-level assistants, business managers—could profit from what these corporate all-stars already knew: remembering names is a wonderful business tool.

It was a heady experience, knowing that my talents could be used not only to entertain but also to help other people achieve their career goals. It certainly wasn't something I had expected.

# Magician Tells All

In my profession, we're not supposed to reveal secrets. But I'm not breaking the magicians' professional code when it comes to the secrets of remembering names and faces. Unlike tricks that are meant solely to mystify and entertain, being able to remember names can benefit people's lives in a way that is truly . . . magical.

*Remember Every Name Every Time* is organized into three parts. The first describes my basic technique for remembering names and faces. It's what scientists call a "left brain"—or verbally-oriented—approach to remembering names. That means it concentrates on the names themselves. The technique also tells you everything you need to know about the best possible way to meet someone so that you'll be certain to hear their name when it's spoken, to clarify that you've heard it correctly, and to cross-reference the name mentally—one of the essential steps in memory-building. The basic technique of Part One is a socially savvy

Benjamin Levy has entertained
and amazed statesmen, heads
of corporations, and royalty
throughout the world.

Few things get by Colin Powell,
but he was relieved of his
watch and was not even aware
of it. Here, Levy returns the
watch, to the Secretary of
State's puzzlement and delight.

approach to remembering names, and one of its outstanding benefits is that it will arm you forever with a reliable and gracious way of meeting strangers.

Part Two reveals my advanced method of remembering names and faces. It's more internal than social, "right brain" rather than "left brain." Here we approach names and faces from a pictorial, imaginative perspective, instead of the verbal, analytic method used in the basic technique. Your memory much more readily retains information that is strange or startling than familiar and mundane. My advanced technique capitalizes on this trait by showing you how to turn an interesting but hardly exciting subject like names and faces into a strange, fascinating and above all *memorable* parade of wild, colorful images. Your eyes are the major sensory portal for your brain, and the secret "language" of the mind is the imagery it uses to make sense of life. I'll show you how to use this "language" consciously as a way of supercharging your memory for names and faces.

The third part of the book is, in effect, a series of briefings for the new memory expert (in other words, *you*):

- How can you apply my techniques when you need to remember not only people's names, but also their titles and the names of their family members?
- What's the best strategy for that awful moment when you *do* draw a blank and fail to remember a name?
- What do some of America's top executives do when they find themselves in that situation?

# Take What You Like

Once you've had even a small taste of success, once you've seen a quick bump up in your ability to remember names and faces, believe me, you'll be inspired to go even further. If not, you'll be so delighted with the improvements that flow just from Part One of my method that you won't feel the need to try Part Two. That's fine. The basic technique is all that some people ever require. I've seen many corporate executives so astonished by its benefits that they don't want to meddle with success.

Others go on to the advanced technique but feel they don't have the time or imaginative energy that's required to make it work. That's fine, too. But if you're game to have a little fun in order to remember names, you'll develop a powerful memory for remembering multiple names for longer periods of time. And keep in mind you're not just remembering abstract names and faces, you're remembering *people*.

No matter how far you choose to go, however, practice *is* essential in getting the most out of what's offered here. The techniques are easy to understand and to execute, but a commitment to practice is required to make them work most effectively. As a magician, I know that a little practice makes tricks good, a lot of practice makes them even better. The same principle applies here—and you don't need a trunk full of props.

# The Ultimate Advantage

There have been many memory-improvement books written before, but few have been devoted solely to remembering names. *And there has never been a book written about the power of remembering names as a business tool.* That's a pity, because while remembering names in a general way is certainly a valuable social skill, it can be a vital attribute in a successful career. As you'll hear from the more than two dozen corporate executives I interviewed for this book, remembering names and faces has a quality that's priceless: it helps you, as they say in corporate offices, to manage up, manage down and manage out.

One of the extra benefits of empowering your memory for names is that your newfound skill will carry over into other parts of your life. You'll soon find yourself putting the techniques to work in any setting where you meet a stranger. Why? Because you'll relish the extraordinarily positive responses you get from people by simply remembering their names when they don't expect it. Think about how absolutely elemental our names are to us. It's one of the first things that newborns hear. Even before they understand language they know sounds, and the sound they hear most often is their own name. Adults invariably ask toddlers, "What's your name?" The first few times a young child answers correctly is an exquisite moment of triumph for the child and the parents.

The first word a child learns to write is his or her own name—another major event of early childhood. Is it any wonder that, as adults, when we hear our names spoken it taps directly into some of the warmest, preverbal recesses of our minds, as if somehow the person speaking it has *understood* us on some elemental level?

There's nothing quite like the effect you can have on other people by unexpectedly remembering their names. They are flattered and impressed with you. They instantly become warmer and more receptive to what you have to say to them. You've probably seen it a few times, or had it happen to you. I've seen the reaction—a delighted, almost childlike elation—literally thousands of times. It's a reaction that cuts across all cultures; nobody's immune to the music of their own name.

But my techniques don't just enable you to remember names and faces. Along the way as they achieve that goal, they also provide you with an entirely new way of meeting strangers. Lots of people go to a cocktail party, a conference reception or even a PTA meeting wondering who'll be there, what they'll say if they get into a conversation and praying for the best. The aim of this book is to provide you with a clear goal going into social situations and an effective way of attaining that goal. As a result, you'll find yourself navigating a roomful of strangers with amazing confidence. And why not? You're carrying a wonderful gift for everyone you meet. *You're going to know their name.* Nothing's more delightful than realizing that someone (you) has taken the time and the trouble to commit their name to memory. (Okay, it's not really much trouble when you're using my techniques, but the other guy doesn't need to know that.) They walk away from meeting you thinking they've made quite an impression, and they have—*just as you've made a terrific impression on them.*

Until now, I've only passed along my secrets of remembering names to my most exclusive clients, senior executives and chairmen of boards of directors. They recognize the value of this seemingly magical ability. Now anyone who has ever longed to have a better memory for names can profit from learning my secrets as well.

## PART ONE

# The Basic Technique

# CHAPTER I

# It's Not Your Fault

The campaign to prevent you from remembering names and faces begins in childhood and only gets worse with time.

"Sometimes when I forget a name, I'll say, 'Oh, I'm having a senior moment.' Or I'll say, 'Gee, I feel very embarrassed.' If you say you're embarrassed, people generally think that's okay. You're saying: You are important to me."

—*Charles Bronfman, Co-Chairman, The Seagram Company Ltd.*

"Don't stare!" How many of us heard that order from a well-meaning parent when we were growing up? "Don't stare!" How many of us have blurted out the same instruction at our own child?

The parental anti-staring policy has the virtue of not making others uncomfortable, but one unfortunate by-product is an early imprinting of the message that we're not supposed to let our glance linger on unfamiliar faces. No matter how indifferent a child might seem to a parent's coaching about how to behave, the actual message reverberates long into adulthood. That's the first reason why your supposed inability to remember faces isn't your fault. Do what everybody else does and blame your parents instead!

Just when a child's world is ready to expand beyond knowing the names and faces of family members, a few friends and cartoon characters, the "don't stare" hurdle discourages adding new names and faces. As years pass, more and more hurdles block the way, doing their insidious work so subtly yet effectively that we blame ourselves instead. "I don't have a good memory for names," we confess, convinced that it's a hopeless case (and unaware that there are techniques for solving the problem). In reality, so much conspires to prevent us from remembering names and faces that few of us ever know how good our memory might be.

Sometimes people cannot remember names for psychological reasons that they're not even quite aware of.

- A friend of mine, a doctor, had such a difficult time remembering the names of his patients that it began to trouble him. Aware of my interest in remembering names and faces, he asked if I could help him. But in the course of our conversation, it gradually became apparent that he wasn't *permitting* himself to remember his patients' names. His specialty was oncology, and his patients sometimes suffered incurable cancers. He realized that he had been blocking out their names as a form of emotional self-protection. Once he came to grips with that issue, I was able to give him some tips that greatly improved his ability to remember names and faces.

- One of the grandmasters of remembering names is someone I've had the opportunity of speaking with on several occasions. We were brought together by mutual friends who assumed the grandmaster would like to meet the new kid on the block—but apparently he wasn't too keen. Whenever we see each other, he can't remember my name. I don't think he's faking it as some sort of professional gamesmanship. I think he literally can't remember my name because he's blocked it out; I'm a rival and competitor and he'd rather I just didn't exist. What better way to make that happen than erasing my name?

- The chairman of a major manufacturing company was having his retirement dinner and we talked about remembering names. I mentioned that I find it easier to remember women's names than men's. "Never could remember women's names," he said. "Why?" I asked, surprised. "I don't know. I guess because they never had it," he replied. "Had what?" I asked. "The power. In my industry over the course of my career they didn't have any power, so I never needed to remember women's names," he replied, adding with a wink, "except when I was young and single."

It's not so much that these people had bad memories for names; rather, on some level they were *choosing* to forget them.

# What's in a Name? Not Much

No small matter here is the problematic nature of names themselves. Names are not good for remembering. Almost every one is a seemingly random cluster of nonsense syllables. Susan? Fred? Bernie? The Pilgrims had a good idea: give people names that are actual, easily remembered words, like Constance or Temperance. Most names today, of the Michael, Tom, or Karen variety, are abstractions that might have fine traditions but don't give you a heck of a lot to work with in remembering them. (Native Americans solved this problem by giving people names when they reached adulthood that evoked their physical or emotional characteristics. Wouldn't it be more helpful to a stranger if my name were Four Eyes, Zero Hair?)

These delicate little syllable clusters called "names" hardly stand a chance of being remembered in the face of the daily avalanche of new information that hits us, oh, starting about 6:30 A.M., when the clock-radio suddenly begins issuing news, traffic reports, weather and last night's sports scores. And that's just while you're trying to pry your eyes open. In the first thirty minutes of your day, the info stream really starts picking up: the newspaper, maybe *CNN* or the *Today Show,* a quick e-mail check, the ingredients on the shampoo bottle in the shower, nutritional information on the cereal box and three things your spouse forgot to mention last night. As the day wears on, the information torrent really kicks in. Voice mail and text messages on your cell phone, faxes, more e-mail, office paperwork, Web sites, more TV, billboards, books (perhaps David Shenk's *Data Smog: Surviving the Information Glut*), magazines, skywriting, movies, snail mail . . . and those two little syllables representing the name of the potential client you met at the bar when you and a few office mates went out for drinks after work. What *was* that guy's name again?

Your brain frantically sorts through all the information hurled at it every day—a single edition of the *New York Times* contains more information than the average literate person in medieval Europe encountered in a lifetime. But unless you develop a strategy for remembering names and faces, they're going to have a hard time gaining a foothold in your memory.

Despite the early-childhood lessons not to stare at the faces of strangers, despite the elusive quality of names themselves, despite the steady crush of new information burying the little ol' name of someone who up until two minutes ago was a complete stranger, you may yet insist: "I have a terrible memory for names." Well, it's *still* not your fault. The modern world has a lot to answer for, not only because the information epidemic has laid siege to our memories, but also because the frenetic pace of contemporary life and the decline of civility has made the old-style formal introduction obsolete.

# The Nonintroduction Introduction

In the more decorous past, every host understood that the purpose of good manners was to put others at ease. Because names and faces are difficult to remember and the prospect of meeting a stranger could be the source of anxiety, an elaborate system of making introductions was developed. The courtly codes of the French and English monarchies a few centuries ago raised the introduction, or being "presented at court," to a level of excruciating formality. One message behind all the pomp was simple: here's the name, here's the face; you're not going to forget it.

In "society," the impulse to go to considerable lengths to ease the meeting of strangers lasted well into this century. Emily Post's detailed writing about the nuances of making an introduction reads like a doctoral thesis on the flight patterns of the monarch butterfly. In Post's bible of manners, *Etiquette in Society, in Business, in Politics and at Home* (1922), the chapter on introductions is broken down into eighteen sections. It begins with "The Correct Form" (use the word "present" on formal occasions, as in "Mrs. Jones, may I present Mr. Smith?"). The chapter moves on through precise instructions in how to speak when making an introduction ("The more important name is said with a slightly rising inflection, the secondary as a mere statement of fact. For instance, suppose you say, 'Are you there?' and then 'It is raining!' Use the same inflection exactly and say, 'Mrs. Worldly?'—'Mrs. Younger!' An example of an improper introduction is: 'Mr. Jones, shake hands with Mr. Smith.' ")

Post must have had an inkling of the coming demise of civility when she set aside a section entitled "New York's Bad Manners." New Yorkers don't have bad memories for names and faces, she complains, they just can't be bothered: "Few New Yorkers possess enthusiasm enough to make an effort to remember all the new faces they come in contact with, but allow all those who are not especially 'fixed' in their attention, to drift easily out of mind and recognition. It is mortifyingly true; no one is so ignorantly indifferent to everything outside his or her own personal concern as the socially fashionable New Yorker. . . ." That certainly rang a bell with this lifelong New Yorker. But it probably holds true in any metropolitan center today.

Mike Bloomberg, the founder of Bloomberg LP, offers an anecdote that updates "New York's Bad Manners." I'll let Mike tell the story himself:

"The other night I went to a dinner party and got there late, just as everyone, about thirty-odd people, walked in to dinner, so I didn't have time to meet everyone. Just by accident, I found myself next to a very famous socialite. This is a woman who kills to have her picture in the papers, and assumes the whole world knows her. So I stuck my hand out and said, 'Hi, I'm Mike Bloomberg.' She said hello, and didn't tell me what her name was. So I said, in a loud voice in front of everybody, 'I'M SORRY, I DIDN'T GET YOUR NAME.' The look of hatred on her face was worth a zillion dollars. It was just great."

Even Emily Post might have been silently rooting for Mike in that situation. And imagine her in another modern setting, the typical suburban party. She walks into a roomful of strangers sitting on sofas and chairs. "Everybody, this is Emily," the host says, munching on a chip and nodding toward her. Then he waves his bottle of Rolling Rock at the gathering and says, "Emily, this is EdKathyBillSarahPeterSusanKevinBarbara." After which some wit pipes up with "You'll be tested on this later," and Emily faints to the floor.

With introductions like that, who needs the voice from childhood saying, "Don't stare!"? You'll draw a blank when trying to connect any name to any face only seconds after this horrific intro is rattled off.

In the unlikely event these days that you're actually introduced to another person in a useful way, there's a good chance that you still won't catch the name—and it *still* won't be your fault. Whether you're meeting someone for the first time in a restaurant, at a cocktail reception, or in a convention hall, it's more than likely that the decibel level in the room is going to make you give up hope of ever hearing whatever the other person says. Unless you're a brilliant lip-reader, the blare of a TV set, a live band, canned music or six other roaring conversations (including someone shouting into a cell phone) is going to make you wonder if the guy across from you just said his name was Tom or Bob or Tum or Blub or Tub or Bum.

You never know where or when the impediments to hearing a name are going to crop up. Economist Marie-Josée Kravis (who, along with her husband, Henry, has engaged me to perform at several elegant dinners), passes along a fascinating tidbit about the challenges in European social settings. Women, it seems, often find themselves mystified about the names of men they meet. "A man bending over, kissing your hand and saying his name—you're just not going to hear it," Marie-Josée explains.

Whether the name's blocked out by a loud band or the fact that it's being spoken into your knuckles doesn't let you totally off the hook about having trouble with names and faces. The reason? It's not your "memory" that's letting you down.

*Some of the blame can be attributed to your own self-consciousness and anxiety about making a good impression.*

When we're on the verge of meeting a stranger, we're so obsessed with trying to present ourselves well, with trying to say something witty or charming—or at least not stupid—that we completely overlook the one thing we can say that will leave the other person thinking we're someone special: his or her name. We don't say it because we might not have even heard it in the first place. But it's just as likely that we've crawled so far into the hole of self-consciousness that we couldn't begin to focus on the other person long enough to hear, or use, their name.

# Iffy Fifty

Worried that you have that medical condition called getting older? Complaints about deteriorating memory increase with each passing year in middle age. But it's not so much that memories get worse as you get older. Researchers are finding that with age the *speed* of memory-recall slows down. Yes, if you think back to yourself as a nineteen-year-old college student cramming for tests and meeting lots of new people, your memory did seem prodigious. Well, in a way it was. It was being primed to remember—and, twenty-four hours later, forget—mountains of factual material. And the new people you met had names that still qualified as almost new to you: how many guys named Gene or girls named Patty had you actually met up until then?

At fifty, you're not cramming for tests and therefore not training your memory to handle bushels of data. And memories seem to lack the vividness they had when you were nineteen, because they do: your eyesight isn't what it was and your hearing isn't as sharp. In many ways, you *have* seen it all. Only something truly extraordinary grabs your memory's attention in the way that a special effect at a rock concert would have blown your mind way back when.

Here's the ultimate reason it's not the fifty-year-old's fault: at that age, the mind is focusing more on the forest than the trees. Big-picture concerns occupy the mind of someone at fifty that a nineteen-year-old can't imagine. Uppermost in your mind at fifty are topics like career, finance and real estate. Why in the world would you assume you should be able to fill your brain with these important matters *and* still be able to remember who won the Oscar for Best Actress last year?

The good news is that being fifty could actually be an advantage in remembering names and faces—if you use the techniques in this book. As you get older, you have more experience of the world, you've met many people who have the same names of the people you meet today. That's great: one of the important steps in memorizing names and faces is cross-referencing the names of new people you meet with names you already hold in your memory. Once you learn to master that technique, you'll be able to give whosis, Mr. nineteen-year-old, a run for his . . . thingamajig.

IT'S NOT YOUR FAULT

# It's Not Your Fault, It's Your Opportunity

No matter how old, or young, or where they are on the road to success, people are invariably perplexed about their self-perceived inability to remember names. And most people feel embarrassed about the lack of this business and social skill. This book will prove to you what is said over and over in these pages. You don't have a poor, horrible, incurably bad memory for names. You just have an *untrained* memory. That's something this book can fix without taking up a great deal of your valuable time and energy. Quite simply, up until now, you didn't have a method to remember names. You just assumed you couldn't.

So please look upon this book as your opportunity to let go of the self-defeating idea that you have a terrible memory for names and use the time you spend with me to hone the good memory you *already* have.

I know you'll succeed. The fact that you haven't acquired these skills is not your fault!

---

External reasons you don't remember:
- Your parents ("Don't stare!")
- "I'm hopeless!"
- Names don't match faces—or anything else.
- Data smog: too much information!
- Unhelpful introductions
- Ambient noise
- You remember the forest, not the trees.
- Self-consciousness

Repeat after me:
- I won't be pessimistic.
- I won't make jokes—even to myself—about my "bad" memory.
- I can do it!

It's not your fault. You don't have a bad memory, it's just untrained.

---

## MAY I PRESENT . . . ?

Entire chapters in books on etiquette have been devoted to the art of making an introduction. Why? Because everyone worries that they're not doing it correctly. I can clear it up for you in a few sentences. It's simple. The sooner we can get people to quit mumbling introductions out of self-conscious worry about getting it wrong, the sooner we'll have people actually hearing each other's names and even, possibly, remembering them.

The basic point to remember in making a good introduction is that you mention the more important person first, the less important person second. I keep it straight in my head by imagining that I'm always introducing the King or Queen to a loyal subject. Not that it would ever come up, but you'd never say, "William the fishmonger, have you met the Queen?" It would be: "Your Majesty, may I present William, purveyor of fish." Or something like that. Big dog: pup; whale: minnow.

Once that's firmly in mind there are three basic lines you can use to make an effective introduction. Look at these three choices, select one that appeals to you. Say it twenty times to yourself and make it your official line of introduction for the rest of your life. Here they are, with the Majesty/peon relationship intact:

- "[Your Majesty], I'd like to introduce [peon]."
- "[Your Majesty], may I present [peon]."
- "[Your Majesty], I'd like you to meet [peon]."

You'll have to sort out, in the social context, who's the royalty and who's the rabble in your introduction. But it's usually an easy call. Majesty usually is: the older person, the woman (meeting a man), the foreign visitor, your boss, the key client. If you're making an introduction between your boss and an important client, the boss gets demoted to peon and the client is crowned Majesty.

Once that opening line is out of the way, *don't forget to give each person one or two pieces of information about the other* so that when you leave, they'll have something to talk about.

# CHAPTER 2

# It's Not Your Fault. Then Again, Maybe It Is . . .

Despite the best intentions to remember names, we often unconsciously sabotage introductions.
Here I am, being subjected to the meeting-and-greeting habits of four highly *in*effective executives.*

"No matter how much memory and power we put into computers, few things are as impressive as someone walking up to you and remembering your name."

—*Ben Rosen, Chairman Emeritus, Compaq Computer Corporation*

## EXHIBIT A: FOCUS ON THE FACE

What we see . . .

What the woman sees . . .
("I hope she's a connoisseur of men's neckwear. . . .")

This woman's body language says: "I'm not terribly interested in meeting you." And that will certainly make sure she misses my name. Maybe it's just shyness on her part. Maybe she feels like there's no point in being attentive because she's not going to remember this person's name anyway. Maybe someone is introducing us and making such a hurried mess of it that she's not even paying attention.

Or maybe it was my cologne.

Whatever the issue was, she has to take charge if she's going to remember my name. She shouldn't interpret a host's bungled introduction as an excuse that lets her off the hook.

She's got to be her own host!

I want to tell her: Greet me and introduce me to your brain—it'll remember me if you just give it a chance.

Instead, she's practically fending me off. Her stiff handshake keeps me out in the cold, beyond gracious proximity. Her lack of a smile isn't good. But her lack of eye contact is a disaster, dooming this meeting to name-recall hell.

## EXHIBIT B: FOCUS ON THE MOMENT

What we see . . .

What the man sees . . .
("Hey, I'm over here!")

This is a friendly fellow. Too bad—he's friendly to everyone but me, it seems. What your mom always said is true: You never get a second chance to make a first impression. And the first impression he's giving off is that he's already looking past me to the next person he wants to meet. The trouble is, he won't get my name, and the next stranger he meets will also be a nameless memory because he's skipping ahead again. If you're going to get a name and remember it, *there must be no more important person in the world to you for the twenty seconds it takes to make your initial contact.*

There will always be lots of distractions in a social setting. The president of the United States has a hundred important things on his mind even when he's navigating through a social event. And yet, George W. Bush and his predecessor Bill Clinton are both noted for their ability to focus on the person in front of them and to make that person feel important. If the president can do it, so can you.

## EXHIBIT C: FOCUS ON THE PERSON

What the man sees . . .
("My name is Benjamin,
not Benjamin.")

What we see . . .

How does my hair look? Is my tie straight? Is that a piece of spinach I feel between my teeth?

Those are just a few of the things this man might have on his mind. He's certainly not thinking about me. Being extraordinarily concerned about presenting yourself well can be the very thing that prevents you from making a good impression. The other person is of secondary concern to the self-concerned individual. When I tell him my name it's going to bounce off the wall of his self-absorption. I'll literally be out of focus to him.

If, like this executive, you know that you can go off the deep end worrying about what people will think of you and how you look, take steps to silence your inner critic. Arrive five minutes early to any event so that you can stop in the rest room and reassure yourself about your appearance. Then charge into the event vowing not to worry about how you look, walk, talk or dress for the rest of the evening.

Get the focus off yourself and onto everyone else.

## EXHIBIT D: FOCUS ON KEEPING IT REAL

What we see . . .

What the man sees . . .
("But enough about me. What do *you* think of me?")

Wow, what a friendly, friendly guy! No more stares at my tie, no more distracted glances over my shoulder, no more self-defeating self-consciousness. This guy's practically delirious to meet me! Check out that eye contact!

So then why can't this "life of the party" remember my name or practically anyone else's?

Because this extra-special greeting is not what it appears to be. It's not the first step in forging a strong personal connection, it's a performance. Everyone he meets gets this standard, over-the-top show. Far from keeping me at arm's length, he's a little too close for comfort. We've just met, but he's already literally in my face. Obviously, his primary interest is in making a dynamic first impression, but it backfires. And it calls to mind the old saying: There are two kinds of people, those who say, "There you are!" and those who say, "Here I am!"

Mr. "Here I am!" tends to walk away from meeting someone else thinking, "Who was that?"

# CHAPTER 3

# Why It Matters

You bought the book. You know this stuff matters. But do you know *why* it matters, or how much? From CEOs to business-etiquette experts, everyone agrees: Remembering names and faces is an essential career tool that can lead to better jobs and higher salaries.

"Sam Walton was great at remembering names. He had mnemonic aids. He had printouts listing every store manager and department head so that when he visited a store he would know them. He had employees wear big name badges: when he went into a store, he wanted to be able to call everybody by their name. He wanted everybody who worked for him to feel like he was their best friend, because that's the way he wanted Wal-Mart customers treated. He was right about all of that. There's no doubt about it—look at the way the company performs."

—*John Huey, editor of Time Inc.'s Fortune Group magazines and coauthor of Sam Walton's* Made in America: My Story

Remembering names creates a warmth that converts new acquaintances into old friends. It's something that I know has been essential to my career. And something many of my clients tell me is integral to running a good business.

# Essential for the Career Toolbox

Now, the reason why one person in the corporate world flourishes and another doesn't is a bit of a mystery, a combination of talent, hard work, good timing, and just plain old dumb luck. But it's an article of faith in business that the ability to remember names is a wonderful tool that can ensure better relationships with clients and open career doors.

The readers of the insurance-industry trade magazine *Life & Health Insurance Sales* know that remembering names and faces is one of the bedrock rules of making a good first impression. Trade magazine *American Salesman* has also advised readers that "clients are flattered when salespeople remember names, and a client who feels important is more likely to place an order . . . nothing is comparable to or more appreciated than remembering and saying someone's name." Everyone acknowledges that remembering names is important. Not everyone thinks it's important for the same reasons—as my interviews with members of America's corporate elite reveal below.

I've already shared with you how vital remembering names has been to my career. And if *you* take the position that remembering names is important to your career, you will actually be able to remember names better. Let me explain. Motivation is essential to making memory work. It sends a signal to the brain that *this is important.* Once you've seen how many different ways remembering names can benefit your life and career, you'll be more deeply motivated to learn my techniques and more successful in putting them to use.

# Corporate Communications

Steven Gluckstern, chief executive officer of Zurich Global Asset Management, tells me that in his view, remembering names is an essential tool both for top corporate executives and for anyone who'd like to run a company one day.

"I think one of the most important characteristics of a CEO, maybe the most important, is the ability to lead," Steven says. "By the time you're a CEO, people are already judging that you're smart enough, most likely, and that you've accomplished enough. What do you do when you get there? You have to lead. Part of being able to lead is being able to connect with people and getting people to follow you. If I say, 'Hey, you, you and you, why don't you come follow me?' why would they do it? You need to motivate people by making a personal connection, and a big part of that is being able to address people by their names."

I couldn't agree more. But then why should someone farther down the corporate ladder bother with remembering names? Steven explains: "Because it may be part of what allows people to display leadership in junior positions and allows them to accelerate and move through the organization more quickly. You don't get to be CEO unless you've exhibited leadership along the way. You must have been doing some of the things that people recognize as part of being a leader." Which would include displaying an ability to remember names and make personal connections.

Sandy Warner, chairman, J.P. Morgan Chase, also homes in on the importance of remembering names as a tool for chief executives. "Connecting with people by name is a very important part of leadership," Sandy tells me. "Making people feel that they belong to a group for which their efforts contribute to something that's greater than the sum of the parts is what leadership is all about. Remembering names adds a dimension that is extraordinarily helpful to getting results."

Time after time when I speak with business leaders, I hear that the ability to remember names is a tremendous career asset. But I've been fascinated to see how many different takes executives have on the subject.

While pointing out various benefits of remembering names, some executives tend to boil it all down to the *role of remembering names in power relationships:*

- Mike Zisman, executive vice president for strategy at Lotus Development Corp.: "If I'm in a conversation with someone I've just met, and they have remembered my name from the introduction and use my name in the conversation, and I didn't remember their name and cannot do that, I am at a disadvantage. That other individual right now is in the power seat. They are showing a lot more finesse. They're able to communicate at a different level than I am because they know my name and I don't know theirs. I've learned over the years that it's very important."

- Bob Hurst, vice chairman, Goldman Sachs: "When I go into meetings and somebody has the facility for remembering names, I find it very impressive. It personalizes the relationship quickly. It makes the person who remembers names feel more in charge and comfortable with people around the table."

Other executives focus on the importance of *remembering names as a means of boosting employee morale and loyalty:*

- Laurence Tisch, co-chairman, Loews Corp.: "If you're in a position to remember the names of a lot of junior people, whose names you wouldn't normally think of remembering, it's a very positive force within a company. I think that it's a big factor in employee morale, when a boss can walk down on a factory floor and greet a person by name."
- Thomas C. Quick, president, Quick & Reilly: "We live in a less and less personal world, so when the officers of a corporation can stop and talk to somebody by name, ask how they are, ask how their family is—that helps in creating an environment that's more effective in retaining valuable employees."
- Dennis Alter, chairman, Advanta: "It's been proven over and over again that, along with fair compensation, the most important factor in employee loyalty and satisfaction is feeling recognized for being a valuable part of the team. That can be reinforced very simply by a senior executive of the company knowing the lathe operator's name. Being able to say, 'Joe, that's great work you're turning out,' is so much more effective than just saying, 'Nice job, way to go, atta boy,' in terms of feedback and increasing the sense of self-worth and self-esteem that people have in their jobs. It may seem like a small thing, but it's enormously powerful."
- Arthur F. Ryan, chairman and CEO, Prudential Financial Inc.: "The war for talent requires every advantage that you can muster. And the more we can do to engage people as something other than as a Social Security number or an object to be directed, the more effective you will be in attracting and keeping the talent you want."

Art says one way that he tries to cultivate the "other than a Social Security number" feeling is to mention people by name while making speeches to employees. "When I give a speech and I say that I'm really pleased with what happened in the development of the new XYZ product, or the new computer system, or the new sales results, if I put a name in there and say, 'I'm really proud of David So-and-so and his group,' it has a much higher resonance than when I just talk about the new XYZ product. If I go lower than David's management level and say, 'Christine So-and-so, who works in David's group, helped develop this.' Then it's not just Christine and David who feel good, but others who've also been involved with the product, even though I didn't name all of them. There's a higher connectivity."

Brad Warner, vice chairman, consumer businesses, at Fleet Boston Financial, agrees that when top managers have the ability to remember names, it translates into increased employee satisfaction. But he takes it a step further, seeing these benefits as ultimately having a positive impact on shareholder value: "My philosophy is based on something called the service-profit chain," Brad tells me. "When you think about the world, you have to think about three things: the customer, the employee and the shareholder. The way to get to the shareholder is to be thoughtful about the value of the services, of the value proposition you give to the clients. That's really delivered day in and day out by the employees. So they have to feel empowered, engaged, connected to that value proposition. You've got to get them excited. If they don't think you know who they are, that's not going to happen. If you create a motivated work force, and you're intelligent enough in your decision-making, you're going to create value for the shareholder."

But it's not all about top executives inspiring the troops. John Huey, editor of the Fortune Group at Time Inc., emphasizes that from his perspective in the office and from observing the business world, the ability to remember names is "hugely important, for managing down, and in managing up, and in managing out."

Here's John on remembering names and managing down: "If you had mastery of this skill, you could use it to make everyone who worked for you, down to the most menial level, feel like you actually cared about them—and you do care, but if you can't remember their name, it's kind of hard to make a convincing case. Imagine the difference, if you were a

Microsoft employee whose name Bill Gates knows and who Bill Gates speaks to by name, or being a Microsoft employee who Bill Gates has never called by name. It's a huge difference."

John on managing up: "It would be useful if you could remember the names of the children and the wives and the secretaries of the important people that you have to stay in favor with to survive in this snakepit that is the American corporate world. I have made it a point in some cases to write down, in my address book, the names of a number of secretaries because they're often more important than the people they work for in terms of getting you what you want. If you don't know my secretary's name and something about her, you'll never get anything out of me because she'll keep you away from me. If you're mean to her, you'll pay for it. If you're nice to her, you'll be rewarded."

John on managing out: "Obviously it's just easier to network effectively if you know who you're trying to network with and those you have already networked with. It could make your life a lot easier. You could be a lot more confident and have a lot less stress in the social interactions that accompany most business activity of any responsibility. If you walk into a meeting knowing everybody's name, and can connect them quickly with faces, then your ability to move through that group with ease is totally different than if you're trying to strategically avoid people because you don't know or can't remember their names. It can freeze you up."

Prepping business people for navigating just those sorts of encounters is one of the main goals of The Lett Group, a Washington, D.C.-based organization that offers instruction in business and social etiquette, international protocol, communications skills, networking and dining skills. In the company's efforts to "teach professionals how to outclass their competition," company principal Cynthia Lett tells me, a particular emphasis is put on the importance of remembering names: "If you really want to get ahead in business, people's names are a major priority. It's absolutely crucial.

"People want to hear their name more than anything in the whole wide world," Cynthia says. "It gets people's attention. It's almost like a compliment every time you say it. They have a feeling in their hearts that you're going to remember them and that this was a positive experience for them. The impression they take away is: 'Wow, I've just made a connection.' It's human nature to want to make connections with one another. When you remember someone's name and use it to their face, that's a very powerful thing."

One aspect of this subject that Cynthia talks about strikes me as especially important to keep in mind. Her clients often don't bother remembering the names of people whom they deem unimportant, she says, but what they don't realize "is that everybody is important to them, because they don't know what is going to come up in the future. This person may turn out to be crucial to their career, or could introduce them to the most important person in their career."

Another expert in corporate etiquette is Dorothea Johnson, director of the Protocol School of Washington, which offers training to men and women from political, diplomatic and business circles in the nation's capital. Dorothea tells me that "management is paying more attention to personal qualities than technical abilities. What I have found in dealing with corporations is that they're looking for executives who are actually like diplomats, who can handle themselves in New York City, in Washington, D.C., in Memphis or in Brussels."

# Presidential Suite

One group of professionals long ago discovered the importance of remembering names and faces: politicians. Every person they meet is a potential "client," a fact that's not lost on many successful candidates for office. In recent times, Bill Clinton gained a reputation as a politician with an almost legendary skill for remembering names.

A journalist friend of mine still talks about the moment in 1991 when she realized that Clinton possessed skills that even seasoned politicians would envy. The young Arkansas governor was running in the Democratic presidential primaries for the first time back then, and met my friend at a campaign stop, chatting with her briefly. In passing, she mentioned that she was trying to find a pay phone so she could call home and check on her young daughter, Lilly, who had an ear infection. The next day, my friend was waiting in line to board a flight home when candidate Clinton rushed through the terminal, obviously late for a flight. "Hi!" he said, greeting my friend by name as he rushed by. Looking over his shoulder, Clinton said, "How's Lilly?"

Another story shows the ex-president's ease with remembering names—and conversely, the trouble his vice president had. An executive I met at a business function where I performed a few years ago told me about her time working in the Pentagon during the Clinton administration. Whenever their paths crossed, the president always said, "Hi, Rebecca." Had her name every time. She knew the vice president better, because her job put her in regular contact with him. That didn't seem to make any difference—the vice president invariably saw Rebecca and said, "Hi, I'm Al Gore."

Now, I'm not saying that his seeming inability to remember names cost Al Gore the presidency, but people skills *do* matter. And the man who beat him in the 2000 election clearly is more gifted in that department. The standard journalistic biography of President Bush always notes that his facility with names and faces dates back at least to his college days at Yale in the 1960s, when he was inducted into the Delta Kappa Epsilon fraternity as a sophomore. One of the methods of hazing new DKE members, in addition to the usual physical tortures, was to demand that they name all of the fifty-five fellow pledges crammed into one room with them. It was a guaranteed form of humiliation—the terrorized sophomores invariably would mumble a handful of names and then endure the disgusted reaction of the other pledges. But when Bush's turn came, he coolly surveyed the room and rattled off every single name. You won't be surprised to learn that he eventually became president of the fraternity.

Since coming into the national spotlight, Bush has also gained a reputation for assigning nicknames to other politicians, journalists, Cabinet members and just about anyone he encounters even on a sporadic basis. Some people are perplexed by Bush's almost compulsive nicknaming, but I suspect it's an inspired tactic. If remembering someone's first name is friendly and flattering, then giving them a nickname and always remembering it is doubly friendly and flattering. Reporters noted that in the first days of the Bush administration, when the new president was mounting a charm offensive on Capitol Hill, he invited members of Congress to the White House and immediately dubbed several of them with nicknames. Rep. Fred Upton (R-Mich.) became "Freddy Boy," for instance, and Rep. George Miller (D-Calif.) turned into "Big George." Miller later heard from a Texas-based reporter that in the Lone Star State, being assigned a nickname by an important person is "like getting the Nobel Peace Prize."

That's certainly reason enough to give out nicknames, making others feel like Texas-style Nobel laureates. But I suspect something else may be at work here: nicknames can also work as a mnemonic device for someone who likes to have a fallback position. If, for an instant, you can't remember someone's name, the fact that they've got a distinctive nickname could help you tap into the person's actual name. A slender acquaintance's name might have slipped your mind, but if you've nicknamed him Lanky Larry, you can *see* his lankiness, which triggers the nickname and leads you to the real name. It sure looks like mnemonics were at work in the 1980s when Bush used an oil-drilling term to nickname a young scientist in his oil-exploration company. Sure, calling someone "Total Depth" has a certain goofy charm, but the nickname also happens to clue the user to the initials of geologist Tom Dickey.

Whatever President Bush's motivation, the value he places on remembering names and nicknames is clearly a reflection of the understanding he gained, as a young man in college and then as a businessman, of one of the basic tools of career advancement. When he brought that skill into the political arena, he joined a long tradition of campaigners who recognized that the best way to get the job is to remember the names of the people who can help you to get it.

How can you make remembering names central to your career success? Turn the page.

# CHAPTER 4

# The FACE Technique: Focus, Ask, Comment, Employ

Follow these four simple steps and you'll never again say, five minutes after meeting someone, "What was that guy's name?"

"When you're introduced to people, if you focus on their name at the time of the introduction, you might remember it. But if you're introduced and you just don't pay any attention, then it's hopeless."

—*Laurence Tisch, Co-Chairman, Loews Corporation*

Admit it. Long before you started reading this book, you tried to *make* yourself get better at remembering names and faces. Maybe it was at a business function when you unexpectedly ran into an influential executive at a company you'd been dying to work for. You didn't know the man, but you *did* know that you wanted to impress him that night. You *had* to remember his name, so he'd be well-disposed toward hearing from you when you called up the next day to explore the possibility of going to work for him.

There he was, standing right in front of you—the guy who might be able to pluck you out of a job you didn't particularly like and plop you down into the one you'd been dreaming about. He said his name was Tom and you were thinking, "Gotta remember it. Tomtomtomtomtom. If I say it enough I won't lose it. Tomtomtomtomtomtom." You could obtain his last name and title from the event organizer. This was going to be great.

A few minutes later, you sensed it was time to move on. You didn't want to look too eager. So you said, "Nice to meet you . . ." and the line died right there. Was it Don? Bob? Tom? Ron? Arrrrgh! Game over. Sure, you could still call the next day to follow up, but the opportunity to sound an effective social grace note, to plant a positive seed in his mind about you—that was gone. How did it happen? You said the name a hundred times! How could you forget Tom? It's such an easy name!

If it makes you feel any better, you could have said the name three hundred times and it wouldn't have done much good. Blind repetition is like continuing to hammer on a nail long after it has already been driven into a board. Ten or twenty or thirty more whacks don't make any difference.

Ever since the first hunter-gatherers started trying to remember the best places for hunting and gathering, humans have been devising ways to improve their memories. Marking a path in the woods would have been about as intricate as memory strategies needed to be in the prehistoric world. But as life became more complex mankind was gradually buried under information that demanded to be remembered. The only solution: mark mental pathways to help find the information. These strategies for remembering are called mnemonics, taken from the Greek word *mneme* meaning "to remember."

One of the most common mnemonic devices is the acronym. This is a collection of letters that spells out a word, which functions both as shorthand for the longer phrase the initial letters come from and also serves as an easy way to remember the phrase itself. Chemistry students use acronyms, such as "C. HOPKINS," for the eight most common elements in seawater (C-carbon, H-hydrogen, O-oxygen, P-phosphorus, K-potassium, I-iodine, N-nitrogen, S-sulfur). One of the simplest acronyms happens to be the one you'd most need in an emergency: people trained in first aid know that ABC stands for Airway, Breathing and Circulation. Sometimes acronyms are unintentionally descriptive. The folks who were working to get Richard Nixon elected to a second term in the White House never could have imagined what a good laugh the nation would get, during the Watergate scandal, from the initials of the Committee to Re-Elect the President: CREEP. Those folks might have done well to keep in mind WASPLEG (the seven deadly sins: Wrath, Avarice, Sloth, Pride, Lust, Envy and Gluttony).

The problem with using acronyms is that too often there's no relation between the mnemonic and the thing you're trying to remember. What were the seven deadly sins—WASPNOSE? WASPNECK? And about those elements, was it B. Hopkins or C. Hopkins? You almost need a mnemonic device to remember the mnemonic device. The closer the acronym can be tied to what it is that's supposed to be remembered, the better the chances are that the acronym—and what it stands for—will be easily recalled. That's why I've devised a name for my basic technique of remembering names and faces that you won't soon forget. It's called FACE, which stands for the four essential steps in the process of remembering names and faces: FOCUS, ASK, COMMENT and EM-PLOY. Each step in the system is grounded in the most current scientific understanding of the way memory works (see Chapter Five). So remember: FOCUS, ASK, COMMENT, EMPLOY. The initials of these four words spell out FACE—the acronym you will use to remember the names and faces of everyone you meet from now on.

## EVERY TIME YOU SEE A NEW FACE, THINK FACE.

The steps will seem simple, even obvious, at first glance—because they are. But taken *together*, they will spur a complex reaction in the mind that makes the recall of a name much more likely than if only one or two or even three steps were followed.

## FOCUS

In sports, they call it putting on your game face. Athletes know that a large part of the battle is getting mentally prepared for their event, blocking out distractions and focusing on the task at hand. Well before the competition begins, they have concentrated their attention on what they're about to do, engaging in what sports psychologists call "positive imaging." When the critical moment finally arrives—a breakaway in a hockey game, a pass into the end zone late in a football game, a pitch with a 3–2 count and runners in scoring position—the athlete is already mentally prepared to handle it, markedly increasing his or her chances of success. Rolf Benirschke, an NFL field-goal kicker for ten years who played for the San Diego Chargers and Oakland Raiders, was accustomed to being thrown into action in the highest-anxiety, game-on-the-line situations. Focus was everything to him. "Instead of being superpsyched at the moment, you slow it down," he once explained. "I used to sing this song in my head: 'Slow down, you move too fast. You've got to make the morning last . . . ' "

Well, business is competition, and meeting strangers is one of the critical moments in the game when you can either score points or get shut out. Slow down, don't move too fast. You can make a lasting impression on another person by establishing a friendly, positive connection. Or you can lapse into the breezy mode that most people use when meeting others for the first time, ensuring that no connection of any usefulness had been made. The most reliable and easiest way to put points on the board is to become proficient at remembering names and faces. The first step toward realizing that goal is to FOCUS.

## FOCUS: PREPARING FOR THE MEET

You can begin to focus well before you're actually heading down the hall into that conference room to meet with potential clients, or parking the car outside the restaurant where a corporate social event is taking place, or riding down the elevator to your company's convention headquarters in a hotel ballroom. Who's expected at the event? If a guest list exists, the event planner probably isn't going to be guarding it like a state secret. If anything, the planner may be flattered that you are interested. Obviously, looking at the guest list in advance will familiarize you with the names of the people you'll be meeting. But the benefits of reviewing the list extend further. First, the simple act of reading it literally makes you FOCUS. It helps you to create a concentrated approach that will carry over to the actual event. Familiarizing yourself with names on the list is also a way of prepping yourself for the next steps in FACE, when you'll need to ASK about the names you want to remember and to COMMENT about them. Knowing in advance some of the names you're likely to encounter lets you get a head start on formulating your questions and comments.

## FOCUS: ASSUME VALUE!

A guest list is nice to have, but it's a bonus in your FOCUS preparation. More important is your mind-set when you meet strangers and try to make the best possible impression. This is where most business people slide into a style of thinking that undermines their chances of successfully remembering names and faces. Their natural shyness may torpedo the operation before it even begins. They see a few familiar faces of coworkers and head over to that group, where they linger for the rest of the evening. Or they dive for the food and drinks tables, and their only words to a stranger are "Have you tried the dip?" When corporations go to the trouble of setting up business-social events, they don't do it out of concern that their employees aren't socializing with each other enough or suffering from malnutrition. They want to see their company representatives building relationships with new clients, cementing ties with existing clients and generally waving the corporate flag. The employee—whether a middle-manager or high-level executive—who confidently extends the company's hospitality to outsiders is almost certain to inspire appreciation from higher-ups.

If you keep in mind the tangible benefits to your career of remembering names and faces it will help you FOCUS. *The more important and potentially rewarding the task seems, the more focused you'll remain.* And the possible benefits of remembering names and faces are far greater than simply earning your boss's gratitude. Is the person who'll hire you for your next big job standing over in the corner, sipping a vodka gimlet? Did a potential client with a multimillion-dollar account just come through the door?

The wonderful thing about meeting strangers is that you never know if the next one is going to have a profound impact on the rest of your life.

*Assume value!*

That's why you should approach each new meeting as an opportunity for career advancement, every stranger as a potential benefactor. Taking that approach will heighten your ability to FOCUS on remembering names and faces—which will help you to become more and more adept at it—thus ensuring that you'll be perfectly prepared. You'll remember

**THE FACE TECHNIQUE**

names and faces as if it were second nature when those life-enhancing opportunities arise.

## FOCUS: BE ALIVE TO THE MOMENT.

This is the critical stage, the moment when you're in the presence of a stranger, seconds away from that first meeting, and then the actual meeting itself. It's where millions of people create the circumstances that make them believe they have "a terrible memory for names." They're so unfocused on the person they're meeting that they never hear his or her name in the first place. Instead, they're mired in self-consciousness, worrying about making a good impression: *Is my hair out of place? I can't shake hands, mine's too sweaty! Quick, think of something witty to say!* In short, they're so focused on themselves that the other person remains a blur. Stephen Covey, author of *The Seven Habits of Highly Effective People,* once told me that people are most fascinated by the fifth habit he enumerates in his book: *Seek first to understand . . . then to be understood.* I can see why—it seems to have life-transforming potential. It also applies to what I'm trying to say here. In obsessing over making a good impression, people overlook the surest possible way of making a *great* impression: *remembering the name and face of the person they're meeting.*

Dr. James L. McGaugh, director of The Center for the Neurobiology of Learning and Memory at the University of California at Irvine, expresses good-natured exasperation with the frequent complaints he hears about the inability to remember names and faces. "Last time you drove your car, do you remember what the car parked next to it looked like? No? You must have a terrible memory for cars," he tells me, chuckling. "People go to a party and the next day they say, 'You know, I just can't remember that person.' The question is: Did you actually look at them? Did you actually get their name when you were introduced? In most cases, no. Most failure to remember names and faces has to do with the fleeting nature of the conditions under which the information is supposedly acquired. The reason why you remember your phone number or your Social Security number is because *you have to.* That's why you figure out ways to do that."

Your job is to combat the "fleeting nature" of meeting new people. The way to do that is FOCUS. Your mind should not be inwardly directed, so preoccupied with making a good impression that you make no impression at all. FOCUS like you're a photographer getting ready to take a picture of your young child and the kid suddenly has the most adorable expression you've ever seen. The moment is going to pass in an instant, never to return, so you'd better FOCUS—perfectly, and *right now.* By FOCUSING on the other person, making a good impression will take care of itself; in the meantime, your memory is receiving pure, invaluable information about his or her name and face. Jerry Lucas, the former NBA star who attained another sort of fame with his astonishing feats of memory, has described how he makes sure that he's concentrating completely on hearing the other person's name and on nothing else. He imagines that his ears are gigantic elephant ears, and they're wrapped around the person he's meeting to be sure he hears precisely what is said.

Once you're actually shaking hands with the other person, it's time for a much more immediate, practical kind of FOCUS. The first task is to get *your* name out of the way quickly. That lets you give your full attention to the person you're meeting. I've found that regardless of whether I'm meeting somebody one-on-one or we're being introduced to each other by a third party, it's helpful to leap into the fray, saying my name and offering a handshake right off the bat. Take control of the exchange. Too often, hosts have never seen a *good* introduction and bungle their attempts. They've had no one to model their behavior after. They mumble people's names or, very unhelpfully, look at John and say, "This is John," and then look at Barbara and say, "This is Barbara," ensuring that John knows he's John and Barbara knows she's Barbara, with neither being quite sure who the other person is. It's not impolite to "help" the host by seeming glad to shoulder some of the burden and introducing yourself.

## FOCUS: THE GOOD INTRODUCTION

I love going to any party hosted by financial writer Andrew Tobias. Andy makes sure that when two people are meeting for the first time, they're both instantly well on the way to getting to know each other. Before I'm even meeting someone, he takes me by the arm, indicating them across the room. Notice how many times he uses the names:

**THE FACE TECHNIQUE**

"See that woman? She's Laura Jones. I want to introduce you to Laura." Then Andy leads me over to this Laura Jones and says, "Laura, may I present Benjamin, Benjamin Levy. Benjamin, this is Laura, Laura Jones. Laura is one of my favorite people. Laura is with Goldman Sachs and she just came back from visiting us in Florida. Benjamin is the greatest sleight-of-hand magician in the country and is working on a book about remembering names. Laura. Benjamin. I'm sorry to leave you but I have to greet the people who just walked in." Then Andy graciously makes his exit, leaving behind two people who feel flattered and who have been introduced as well as anyone's going to be in this day and age.

If no host is on hand and you're meeting a stranger, introducing yourself and shaking hands has the advantage of getting your own name out of the way so that you can FOCUS. It also ensures that the other person will say his or her name, too, instead of just saying, "Hi." *When the stranger answers, this is the moment you've been priming yourself for.* The information that's about to be offered is gold for you. Don't choose that moment to scan the room to see if there's anyone more important around (in fact, don't do that at any point during your exchange, unless you'd like to have your name and face remembered as belonging to someone worth avoiding). If you're in a party setting with music playing or a steady, loud buzz of conversation, lean closer to hear the name as it's uttered. Make eye contact, but glance at the other person's lips as they say their name—you want to make sure that you catch the name correctly the first time, even though it's going to be useful to pretend not to have heard it clearly. One executive I know goes so far as to have a policy of never letting go of a handshake until he's sure he's heard the other person's name correctly. Which brings us to the next step of FACE.

The essentials of maintaining FOCUS:
- Be prepared.
- Assume value.
- Focus on the other person, not on yourself.

## ASK

Even if you've focused on hearing the name and are positive that you heard it correctly, it's crucial to ask to hear it again anyway. First of all, despite your certainty that you heard it clearly, you'd be surprised by the number of different ways names can be mis-heard. Consider the pernicious *similarity* of men's names. In a crowded room full of chattering people, hearing the differences between Tom, Don and John can be almost impossible. Then there's the pernicious *lack of similarity* between the ways that people with names spelled the same actually pronounce them. We all know a Diane who pronounces her name "Dee-ann," or a Sandra who pronounces it "Sondra." (That's why name badges give a false sense of security. You didn't quite hear what she said, but her name badge clearly says it's "Joanne." Well, I happen to know a Joanne who insists that it's pronounced "Joan.") And don't get me started about names that sound precisely the same but are spelled differently. Gene, meet Jean—the former named for his dad, Eugene, the latter the Americanized son of a French-Canadian couple. In a perfectly quiet room, you can still not get the name right.

*Any* name, then, bears a second hearing. And it's certainly better to make the confirmation while meeting someone rather than waiting until you run into the person ten minutes later. In the first case you're saying you didn't catch the name, in the second you're admitting that you've forgotten—a huge difference.

But clarification is only part of the reason why you need to ask the other person to repeat his or her name. ASK is the second step in the process of remembering names and faces, a process scientifically designed to establish as many new neuron strings in the brain's memory center as possible, maximizing the likelihood you'll remember the name. Each step in FACE feeds this new name to the brain in a different way, so it's vital not to skip ASK before moving to the next step. Some people are tempted to move on to the next step, though, because they feel uncomfortable with ASK. Nevertheless, if you want to get this right, follow these steps and don't just ask the other person to repeat the name, but ask several questions pertaining to the name, like how to spell it. Even though you may not be happy to play the inquisitor, it's vital.

I remember giving a private lesson to one CEO, in his stunning office overlooking Manhattan's Central Park, when he suddenly roared at me, "Dammit, I can't be seen asking people all these questions!" He was wrong. But there was one occasion when I dearly wished I had agreed with him. It was in the 1980s, when I was starting out in my career by performing tableside for well-heeled diners in restaurants. I had already discovered the value of remembering names back then. I developed a few memory tools and had even taught them to a friend of mine, Hollywood screenwriter Chris Soth. One night when I was performing, Chris was waiting for me at the bar. He fell into conversation with a group of five women. Chris and I were both single, so when I finished my work I was delighted to see Chris waiting for me surrounded by an attractive female quintet. I *really* wanted to remember their names. "Is that Meryl, M-E-R-Y-L?" I asked the first one. Yes, she said, looking oddly at me, as if she thought I was going to say, "As in Streep?" The next woman was Diane. "D-I-A-N-E?" I spelled out (I'm always worried about those Dian*n*es lurking out there.) She said yes, but I thought she almost laughed for some reason when she said it. "I'm Tracey," the next woman interjected, adding immediately, "T-R-A-C-E-Y." Then she looked at Chris—whom I had just tutored that afternoon in remembering names and who had used the technique in getting to know these women minutes before—then she looked at me, turned to her friends and said with appalled incredulity, "They're *spellers.*"

Okay, so if millions of people read this book and start putting FACE to work, there may be a lot of *spellers* out there. But there are lots of ways to ask and ask again. Far from seeming like you're badgering the witness, to most people it will seem extremely flattering.

## ASK: THE CLARIFICATION

Self-deprecation is a terrific social tool; people are happy to help out if you say after a hurried introduction, "I'm sorry, that went by too fast for me. Was it Robert?" There are plenty of variations on this, if you're meeting one-on-one: "I'm sorry, did you say Robert?" "It's so loud in here! Was that Robert?" "I didn't catch that—did you say Robert?" "My hearing's awful. Was it Robert?" Or how about the perfectly good, perfectly simple: "Robert?" Notice that in every example here, you're speaking the name aloud. This is important. Just blurting out, "What did you say?" will succeed in getting the other person to repeat his or her name. This, however, diminishes the value of asking the question because you've lost an opportunity to speak the new name out loud yourself. (Note: people often tend to swallow the first part of their names, and listeners often don't focus in time to hear it anyway. I can't tell you how many times I've asked "Ed" to say his name again, or said "Is that Ed?" and found out that his name is Greg. Or Fred. And Linda turns out to be Belinda or Melinda.)

ASK's goals are twofold: to make certain that you've heard the name correctly, and to drive the name into your brain's memory center as deeply and in as many different ways as possible. Hearing Robert speak his name again is helpful, *but the real payoff is when you say it out loud, too.*

Of course, this is all contingent on your meeting taking place under common circumstances—a convention center, a reception, a hotel lobby—where there's lots of ambient noise. If you're meeting in the hushed confines of a conference room, saying, "John? Did you say it was John?" will just seem bizarre. If you're meeting in a quiet zone, forget Clarification and skip ahead to:

## ASK: THE ELABORATION

Your first question establishes whether the name you thought you heard in the FOCUS stage is in fact the other person's name. Further, it gives you the chance to speak the name out loud. The process of reinforcing the name in your memory, and of reintroducing it in different ways, has begun.

Now it's time to move to a second line of questioning, which will more deeply implant the *newly acquired name information* in your brain. It's a delicate art, asking people about their names: there's a fine line between sounding curious and sounding like a stalker. Be careful to keep your tone light, not urgent.

One of my private clients reported back to me an approach that I had never thought of—and I think it's a wonderful way to accomplish the goal of converting an initial meeting into a conversation about the other person's name. Whenever he met someone new my client said, "I'm reading a book about remembering names. Can you tell me about yours?" As it happened, he *wasn't* reading a book about remembering names, he just needed a way to steer the conversation in that direction (sometimes, for variety, he'd say, "My new hobby is remembering names. . . .").

Well, you really *are* reading a book about remembering names. When you're done, you will have *just read* a book about remembering names. Let that be your hook for ASKING about the other person's name.

Trust me, people almost invariably respond positively when asked for details about their names. It's flattering. People like to have attention focused on them.

There are many follow-up questions that you can ask after hearing a stranger's name. You can almost pretend that the other person has asked you to inscribe a book and you want to make sure you have the name down precisely:

- "Is that Kathy with a K or Cathy with a C?"
- "Do you prefer to be called Robert, or is it Rob or Bob?"
- "Should I call you Bill, or is it always William?"
- "Is that A-n-n, or A-n-n-e?"
- "My friends are having a baby boy and they're thinking of naming him Ed. How has it been being an Ed?" *(I've found that when I'm at a loss for anything else to say to someone I've just met, this can be a lifesaver.)*

You can also ask about family connections if, at that time, it seems appropriate ("Dahlia, like the flower. I've never met someone named Dahlia before—is there a special reason your parents chose it?").

If you're meeting several people in succession, you'll want to vary the questions so that you don't sound like a census-taker. The more commonplace John, Bill, Mary and Karens of the world will naturally elicit your most *general* questions. But there are many people out there with unusual names. Perhaps they're the offspring of 1960's flower children named Sunshine or Rainbow, or from foreign countries where every name sounds exotic to you—then you can get specific and the questions should come to mind very easily. "Layla—I'm guessing your parents were Eric Clapton fans?" Or: "I want to remember you but I don't quite get your name. How do you spell Sveinung?"

Obviously, you'll need to tailor the question to the name involved—asking David how he spells his name is going to sound strange, but I find that if, once I've started talking about names with someone I've just met, I say, "My grandfather's name was Benjamin," then it's not at all odd to ask, "Were you named after someone, David?" Solid, traditional names can have some family history behind them.

Notice that in all of the sample questions above, I've taken care to include the person's name. Like the first step in ASK, when you take advantage of clarifying what the person's name is to repeat the name, the follow-up questions offer you a chance to speak the name aloud still another time. Repetition is a key to consolidating any memory, so try not to ask a question like, "Are you named for a relative?" without including the person's name. But the main goal here is to turn the conversation, if circumstances permit, into *a conversation about the name.*

## ASK: THE BALLAD OF SY AND TERRY

I was recently visiting my father, Sy, and mother, Suzanne, in the Berkshires of western Massachusetts, where they retired to several years ago. My father and I went out to lunch at one of his favorite local spots. On the way over, we had been discussing this book and the whole topic of remembering names, so when we slid into our booth and the waitress came over, he said to her, "You know, I've been coming here for six years and I've never asked your name. What is it?" The waitress smiled, seemingly flattered by his interest, and said, "Terry."

My dad introduced himself and me, and he was about to start looking at the menu. But I couldn't let it stop there. I asked the waitress, "I suppose Terry is short for Theresa?" Ninety-nine times out of a hundred, it's short for Theresa. This was the other one: "No, actually my name is Terecita." *That* was interesting—I'd never met a Terecita before! It touched off a whole discussion about her mother and how she came here from Cuba. All the while, my father listened in amazement at the amount of family history spilling out of this woman he had spoken with dozens of times but never really knew.

Believe me, by the time we left, neither one of us would ever forget the waitress named Terry. All because we took the trouble to ASK about her name.

## ASK: THE SECRET AGENDA

While you're asking for more information about the name of the other person, a lot more is going on than just creating an opportunity for you to

**THE FACE TECHNIQUE**

speak the name aloud and to clarify particulars about its spelling or origin. Inside your brain new neuron strings are firing every time the name is spoken and with the arrival of every new piece of information about the name. And you're also secretly conducting a reconnaissance mission on behalf of the next step in FACE. Because that step calls on you to COMMENT in connection with the name, the questions posed in ASK can be extremely helpful in providing fodder for the COMMENT. That's why I encourage you not only to ASK, but also to ASK again. Simply asking about the spelling of a name doesn't extract much information that will be useful for COMMENT. Finding out about other aspects of the name, like the story behind how someone's parents selected the name, or its ethnic origin, will be of real value to you during this next phase.

---

Reasons for ASKING:
- Confirm that you heard the name pronounced correctly.
- Clarify the spelling.
- Discriminate between the full name and its diminutive.
- Ask for more information—flattery will get you everywhere.

---

**EVERY TIME YOU SEE** **THINK FACE.**

## COMMENT

As you'll see in the discussion of the scientific aspects of FACE in the next chapter, *the crucial aspect of memory-building is the forming of connections between new information and things the brain already knows.* Cross-referencing helps embed the new info. A tenuous bit of previously unfamiliar fact will quickly be forgotten unless you can tie it to existing strands of knowledge in your brain. Think of a new name coming into your brain with several bungee cords dangling free, their hooks ready to be snared by permanent mounts already waiting in your brain. During the FOCUS and ASK stages in FACE, you've managed to hook a few of the bungee cords onto the surface of the brain. Focusing on the importance to your career of remembering names, concentrating on the name as it's spoken, asking if you heard it correctly, asking again about the name—all of these actions have the effect of latching down another mental cord that will make it difficult to dislodge the name from your memory. The cords are like the neuron strings coursing through the brain's memory center, strengthening the ties between the name and your ability to recall it.

Making one of the most crucial ties of all is what you accomplish with COMMENT. This takes the name deeper into your memory by linking it to knowledge that is already rock-solid in your brain. The name's much less likely to slip away if it's moored to a secure base in your memory.

## COMMENT: THE TALKING CURE

At this point in the FACE process, you've FOCUSED on hearing the name and ASKED about it in at least one way (in the optimum situation, you've had a brief conversation about it). The basic information has been established. This new name is becoming linked more strongly in your memory with the face in front of you. It's an appropriate moment in the conversation to make a COMMENT that follows on what you've just been talking about: *the other person's name.* Saying something that's pleasant, amusing or informative is socially graceful at this juncture. The other person will have appreciated being the center of attention, but will also appreciate hearing something from you that will give him or her an opening to say something equally pleasant, amusing or informative. I don't mean to make this process sound like particle physics—we're talking about *chatting,* for heaven's sake. But it helps to make clear precisely what's going on in these interactions. How else to control their outcome to your benefit?

The most likely topics to comment about will flow directly out of the information you've elicited with ASK. If John was named for his father and his grandfather, you might say, "Let me guess, your son's name is . . . Bob?" and then mention the entertaining factoid that ex-boxer George Foreman got carried away and named *all* of his children—about ten of them at last count—George.

I met a woman named Pia recently, and I said, "Now that's a great name. I don't meet many Pias." That sparked a whole back-and-forth conversation about the name Pia. I then told her that I seemed to recall an actress named Pia Skala (I was wrong, I realized later—it was Lillia Skala—but at least it kept the conversation moving). She said that people often mention Pia Lindstrom, Ingrid Bergman's child from her first marriage and a longtime fixture on local TV news in New York City. To which I replied, "And there's always Pia Zadora," which got a laugh. It was an easy exchange, much more enjoyable than talking about the weather—and it created an avalanche of new connections in the memory center of my brain. The message "Pia, Pia, Pia" was zapping into my mind over several different routes, tying into areas related only by the name itself (I don't know about you, but I file "daughter of Ingrid Bergman" (Pia Lindstrom) in a folder totally separate from that of the "actress from *Naked Gun 33⅓*" (Pia Zadora).

Your COMMENT doesn't have to be the catalyst of a whole conversation. Sometimes the only thing that will occur to you is a simple statement of fact: "My brother's name is Simon, too," or "Melissa—that's my wife's name." You're not playing Ted Koppel here, or Oprah Winfrey—the onus isn't exclusively on you to keep the conversation going. Your COMMENT is intended primarily to give you the opportunity to say the name aloud again, and to make a connection between the name and an existing memory within your brain. COMMENTING about your name and their name offers information that gives the other person something to respond to.

A word here about making a humorous COMMENT. If you're a naturally funny conversationalist, give it a shot. But be aware that people are naturally protective of something so personal as their own names. If you encounter Denise and feel absolutely positive that it's going to go over big if you say, "Pleased to meet you, Denise. I just met de nephew over there," then by all means quip away. The reality is that by the time most of us have gotten past sixth grade, we've heard just about every joke imaginable about our name and aren't going to be particularly amused to hear one of them revived. That's not to say that you can't *think* of a joke—just keep it to yourself. Which brings us to . . .

## COMMENT: THAT VOICE IN YOUR HEAD

Okay, I came up with a mnemonic device—the acronym FACE—so that when you see a new face, it triggers the steps of my basic technique for remembering names and faces. Now it's your turn to come up with a simple, memorable connection to any new name that you want to remember. This will be a mental COMMENT you'll make in the course of your meeting—just a simple form of word association—that links the name to the same one that already exists in your memory bank. It's important for this to become almost reflexive when meeting someone—so much so that I recommend simply having a policy that whenever you hear a new name, you automatically think, "Like . . . ," which will lead you to something you already know that's related to the name.

Here's the sort of dialogue using FACE that I'm talking about:

> I meet a stranger. I say: "Hello, I'm Benjamin."
> Stranger: "I'm Alex."
> BL: "Alec?" (I'm thinking: Like . . . Alec Guinness? Like . . .
> Alec Baldwin?)
> Alex: "No, short for Alexander."
> BL: "But you like Alex, not Alexander? I just ask because I like
> Benjamin, not Ben."
> Alex: "Yes, please call me Alex."

Now, during the ensuing conversation, I'm riffling through my mental database of others named Alex or Alexander. The history buff hears "Alexander" and thinks "Like . . . Alexander Graham Bell, Like . . . Alexander the Great." The sports fan thinks of quarter-billion-dollar star Alex (A-Rod) Rodriguez. The TV trivia buff thinks of Alex, the Michael J. Fox character on *Family Ties,* or *Jeopardy*'s Alex Trebek. The musically inclined remembers "Alexander's Ragtime Band."

You might associate the name with a politician, an actor, a singer,

**THE FACE TECHNIQUE**

a line of poetry where the name occurs, a character in a novel, a name in a song title—your own particular experience of the world will dictate what springs to mind when you hear a name. *You're mentally cross-referencing the new information with something you already know.*

Or suppose you're meeting someone named Barbara. Bingo! Singer Barbra Streisand; former First Lady Barbara Bush; Barbara Billingsley, or Mrs. Cleaver, to *Leave It to Beaver* fans; actress Barbara Stanwyck (*Double Indemnity* and TV's *Big Valley*); California Senator Barbara Boxer; the Beach Boys' song "Barbara Ann."

You see? Almost any name, unless you're meeting a group of executives from Indonesia, or Iran, or some other non-European country, can stir a memory of the same name in a much different context. The more you become familiar with names and interested in them, the greater your *vocabulary of names* will become. The connections will come more easily and in greater numbers because a certain section of your mind is teeming with them. A tennis player has his repertoire of shots, a ballet dancer her array of steps. You need a reservoir of names. (When confronted with unusual names you've never encountered before, put special emphasis on ASK. Make sure you've got the spelling right and otherwise amp up your concentration because you won't have a mental COMMENT available to provide extra emphasis.) Taking a moment to remark mentally on the connection will help to drive home this new name and face, because it's being linked to a memory already securely lodged in your mind.

Your mental COMMENT may just be as simple as "Oh, Alex like in *Family Ties.*" That's something you wouldn't say out loud, but it's sufficient to activate a neuron-string tie between the new name and your more permanent memory. Some comments will work if you say them aloud: a politician or a banker named Alexander probably won't mind your mentioning the politician and star of the ten-dollar bill, Alexander Hamilton.

Whether mental or spoken aloud, the COMMENT adds another level of connectedness that will make it easy, when you run into Barbara at the elevator an hour or two after meeting her, to say, "Barbara, can I give you a call tomorrow about that new product we were talking about?" Getting off the elevator, you might even find yourself singing, "People, people who meet people . . ."

## EMPLOY

Despite the attention you've paid to the other person's name so far in the conversation, you haven't actually used it yet in a natural, friendly way that reflects the familiarity you've established with this new business contact. You've spoken the name inquisitively ("Did you say Ed?" "It's Ed?" "You prefer Ed to Edward?") You've used the name in referring to another person ("My father's name is Ed. My mother's the only person in the world he allows to call him Eddie." Or: "I used to vow that when I grew up I'd name my son Ed—because I worshiped Ed Kranepool on the New York Mets"). But you've never just spoken his name casually in a way that signifies both to yourself and this new acquaintance that you've fully integrated it into your memory. It's time to EMPLOY the name, which will build yet another new memory pathway in your brain.

And why not EMPLOY the name? It's as if you've already put an individual name itself through the interview process. The first three steps in FACE amounted to vetting a job applicant, FOCUSING closely when it came through the door, ASKING questions about the name's background and origins, COMMENTING in a way that established some common ground. Now imagine that you've hired the name; it's an EMPLOYEE waiting to go to work for you. The name's job is essentially to close the deal for you, to put the finishing touches on its place in your memory.

### EMPLOY: CAREFULLY

Don't be a slavedriver. EMPLOY the name judiciously—just a couple of graceful appearances in your conversation, probably toward the end, will be an adequate brain exercise. So far, all the information has been pouring into the memory center in a variety of ways; the final test is to see if you've mastered the name so well that you can pop it into conversation like you're chatting with an old friend. Going overboard here doesn't help, and may be off-putting. One way to EMPLOY without becoming annoying is to do it *internally* as well: If you and your spouse are talking to someone you've just met, EMPLOY the name mentally: "The man talking to my husband is Rick." But you still need to EMPLOY the name out loud—and it's a rare person who can repeatedly use in conversation the name of someone they've just met and not sound like a third-rate salesman. It creates a false intimacy that makes the other person squirm. (When Catherine answers your question by saying that she actually prefers to be called Cathy, there's no need to say, "Oh, really, Cathy?" That's when you risk straying into weirdoland.) A serial name-user hurts his cause more than he helps it by chattering away with transparent gambits like, "What do you think about those Baltimore Ravens, Don?" "Don, is the weather cold enough for you?" "That's a nice watch you're wearing, Don."

In contrast, you've already expressed an open interest in knowing the person's name and finding out more about it. You haven't deployed it in the haphazard way of a backslapping Willy Loman, but you haven't EMPLOYED it, either. That's why working it into your conversation toward the end is such a good strategy: it cements the name in your memory, yet is subtle enough that it strikes the other person as proof that you're a polite, considerate person with an interest in them.

## EMPLOY: THE JOB DESCRIPTION

Here's what I'm talking about. Presumably after you've passed the COMMENT point in the conversation, the two of you have moved on to other topics—the reason why you're there for your company, how business is going, gossip about hirings and firings in your sector of the business world. When the conversation approaches its natural conclusion after a few moments, as is the nature of these encounters at cocktail parties, corporate dinners or convention get-togethers—it's entirely appropriate for you to EMPLOY the other person's name. "Do you need a refill, Kevin?" "Have you tried any of the food yet, Kevin?"

This may be just my prejudice, but I prefer to use the name at the end of the sentence rather than at the start. Putting it first sounds a little too urgent (unless you're using it as a casual attention-getter, as in Kevin's talking to someone else, you're heading to the bar and you say, "Kevin—can I get you a drink?"). Attaching it to the end sounds friendlier, like more of an afterthought. It implies that you're so familiar with the name that it can just tag along with whatever you really wanted to say. Nobody will notice that the name is actually your EMPLOYee, toiling away to strengthen its place in your memory.

Maybe the best way of using the other person's name in conversation is in the third person. You're talking to a few people, Kevin among them, and you say, "As Kevin just said . . ."

Bringing an end to the conversation presents the last chance to EMPLOY the name casually. An especially effective way of doing this is to introduce him to someone you already know (or whom you met earlier and whose name you used FACE to remember!). "Gail, have you met Kevin? Kevin's working over at Tech-Scan Communications."

But here's the simplest, most straightforward exit strategy, one that also has the advantage of bundling together both a compliment and the feel-good effect of letting the other person hear his name: "It was nice meeting you, Kevin."

*I hope that once you've mastered these four steps, whenever you meet someone for the first time, seeing a new face will instantly trigger putting the FACE technique into action.*

---

Try to EMPLOY the other person's name in any one of four ways:
- When possible, make the other person's name the topic of your initial conversation.
- Use it once in the course of talking.
- Introduce the person to others.
- Say goodbye using the name.

---

**EVERY TIME**
**YOU SEE**                        **THINK FACE.**

# The FACE Technique in a Photographic Nutshell

One of the fastest ways to learn is to model successful behavior. Do what an expert does and you'll reap the same benefits—without all the tedious grunt work. Here's the essence of the FACE technique (pardon my silent-movie-actor mugging).

"I'm Benjamin Levy, and you are . . . ?"

## STEP ONE: FOCUS

When you truly FOCUS on the person you're meeting, she gets a positive message from you. She sees and feels that: "This guy's paying attention to me. He's interested in me. He's making an effort."

What I'm doing in the photo is almost literally giving the other person my ear. I'm giving this meeting my all. There is nothing more important to me in the whole world at this moment than getting your name. You're throwing a baseball to me at 98 m.p.h., the crowd is screaming and I'm determined to catch it.

None of the other steps in FACE will fall into place if you don't put everything you have into catching the name by FOCUSING.

Don't drop the ball!

Experts in body language agree that you can convey a very positive message in your pose. Note what I'm doing in the picture.

"Cathleen?" "Yes." "That's amazing! Just yesterday, I got business cards from three women named Cathleen, all spelled with a 'C.' Do you spell it with a 'C'?"

"No, it's with a K." "Oh! Like . . . Kathleen Turner."

I'm leaning forward.

My body position is open and receptive.

I'm touching the other person by shaking hands.

I'm riveted. My eye contact at this point is unrelenting.

I'm FOCUSED.

## STEP TWO: ASK

I'm asking to clarify that I've heard the name correctly. This will engage my mind and further activate my memory process. I'm getting involved with the name. And the side benefit is that Cathleen notices that I am genuinely paying attention—I really care.

## STEP THREE: COMMENT

Complete clarity achieved! Now I recognize precisely what her name is and how it's spelled. And I've cross-referenced it with an actress's name I'm already familiar with (if you prefer, you can make your cross-referencing COMMENT simply a mental note to yourself). The actual flash of recognition for me provides an emotional involvement that helps to make this meeting memorable.

You will be amazed when you see that someone with even a slightly unusually spelled name is nearly as impressed by your "getting" the spelling as they will be if you later remember the name itself.

**THE FACE TECHNIQUE**

## STEP FOUR: EMPLOY

"Kathleen, I'd like to introduce Jim."

A terrific aid to your memory is taking new material and teaching it to someone else. That's what occurs when you introduce someone you've just met to a third person. It also gives you the opportunity to speak the new name aloud, which further fixes the memory in place. To this end, don't forget to use the other person's name again as you close the conversation: "It's been a pleasure to meet you, Kathleen."

All of this might sound like common sense. But it's not common practice. Use all four steps of FACE and you will *never again* meet someone and five minutes later say, "Now what was her name?"

# CHAPTER 5

# Memory, FACE and Science

The components of FACE—Focus, Ask, Comment, Employ—were designed not to force you to learn a new way of remembering, but to get the fullest benefit from the way your mind naturally works.

"To speak a person's name is to invite relatedness, to signal recognition of that person's unique existence. As Freud said, 'A man's name is a principal component of his person, perhaps a piece of his soul.' Or as the *Cheers* theme song had it, we all long for a place where 'everybody knows your name.' "

—*Psychoanalyst Dr. Fredric T. Perlman*

You've learned the FACE technique. You might have even already tried it out and had some success. That's exciting, but probably a little mystifying—it's one thing to understand that a technique works, but another to understand *why* it's so effective. Matters of the mind can often seem like magic even to neuroscientists, who acknowledge that they've only skimmed the surface of understanding how the brain functions. But researchers are beginning to divine at least the outlines of the way memory works, and their findings help to explain why FACE can erase that age-old complaint, "I've got such a bad memory for names and faces."

Before moving on to the next, more advanced section, it's important to understand the scientific rationale for approaching memory in this way. Anyone can lift weights and improve his or her physical strength, but the weight lifters who learn about anatomy and the physiological basis of their workouts often get the most out of their sweat sessions in the gym. Similarly, you can simply practice FACE and its advanced form and strengthen your ability to remember names and faces. But if you understand *how* my approach taps into the science of the brain, you'll realize the importance of every step. That will help you to get the most from your memory workouts. In addition, seeing how FACE meshes with the science of the mind will establish that my approach isn't based on some kind of mental trickery that provides unreliable results; it's as certain to improve your remembering ability as the steady use of a Nautilus machine is to tone your muscles.

# Memory's Gatekeeper

The crucial player in the making of memory is a rippling curve of tissue deep at the brain's center called the hippocampus, named after the Latin word for seahorse because of its arching form. This is where the brain pencils in the encyclopedic flurry of information we receive every second that has the potential to become a memory. The hippocampus gives the thumbs-up or thumbs-down to the info—yes, remember shaking hands with Tiger Woods, no, don't remember shaking the catsup bottle over your fries at lunch an hour later—and the process of memory-making begins.

Of course, the hippocampus rejects most of the information it receives from the cerebral cortex because so much of our daily experience doesn't remotely merit being retained. The information has a fleeting existence as a perception created by the senses, and then simply vanishes. Walking up steps, feeling a breeze, noticing an ant on the porch—these are momentary, not momentous events. An "immediate memory" lasting less than a minute is formed, but it's just a flash in the brainpan unless it spurs a positive response from the hippocampus. If that happens, a memory starts to take shape—literally—because the formation of memory is a physical process. The cerebral cortex overlays the brain with ten billion strings of nerve cells, which transmit information by sending chemical and electrical impulses. Every time a sight or sound or any other perception enters the brain, a unique array of these nerve cells, or neurons, is activated. If the perception doesn't carry any significance other than letting you know that, say, you have successfully completed tying your shoes, the perception goes *poof!* and the specialized neuron network it inspired then resets, waiting for the next spurt of input.

# A String Symphony

If the perception carries valuable information—yes, those really are the winning numbers on your lottery ticket!—the hippocampus alerts the cortex: *don't let this one get away.* Immediately, the singular neuron pattern spurred by the perception solidifies, the connections between the neurons are strengthened, and a usable network falls into place. The emphasis here is on the word usable: use the network or lose it. The pattern will fade back into the general neuron population if it isn't called into action. But recalling the information repeatedly, in a variety of contexts, strengthens its perch in the cortex. Not that this memory sits in any single spot in the brain. Several different regions of the mind contribute to the whole presentation of a memory—which is why memories are best retained by "encoding" them in a variety of ways.

Now, how does the hippocampus go about deciding what information to reject for encoding and what deserves free parking on memory lane? I like to think of the hippocampus as a booker for the Jerry Springer TV show: it goes for the emotional and the sensational. That person you just fell in love with at first sight will get the red-carpet treatment from the hippocampus when he or she finally says, "Hi, my name is . . ." The more vivid the hippocampus-bound info the better, too. It's not just extreme events, like being in a car accident, that are more likely to get the okay. Even narratives of stories you're not involved in make a deeper memory impression.

Researchers at the University of California, Irvine, noted this in 1994 when they related a story with varying details to volunteers and then queried the listeners about what they'd heard. In one version of the story, a mother and her son are going to visit Dad and pass a junkyard along the way. In another form of the story, the kid is hit by a car. Guess what? The volunteers remembered the accident-marred story much more clearly than they recalled the mundane version.

# Haven't I Seen You Somewhere Before?

Another influence on the hippocampus is whether or not new information strikes a chord with something that's already familiar. The brain is constantly on the lookout to make associations with things already in its memory bank. People often draw comparisons between the way computers work and brain function, and there are indeed parallels. A computer's RAM (random access memory) resembles the brain's minute-to-minute working memory. They both involve using functions that allow the computer or person to operate effectively—like saving a file or saving five cents by using a coupon at the grocery store—without calling into action the hard drive or long-term memory. And our long-term memory is, in effect, our hard drive: memories are inscribed in our brains by neuron code much the way that hard drives are crammed with digitally coded "memories." But computers are just crude approximations of the human brain, lacking the exquisite, confounding beauty of the way our minds navigate us through life. *One major difference between the two is the brain's constant yearning to make associations between what it already knows and what it's learning.*

Let's say that you've already set aside a lot of neural memory-strings to knowing an exhaustive amount about the mating habits of the South American tapir because that's what your doctoral dissertation was about. When the science section of the *New York Times* runs a tiny item announcing a discovery about the romantic lives of tapirs, the news won't make any impression on ninety-nine percent of readers. But your hippocampus will pounce on the information, prompting the brain to weave it into the tapir-related data already grouped together in the cortex.

So the hippocampus sifts through the deluge of potentially memorable input it receives every day, generally looking for information that either has some emotional significance, carries a sensational quality (you can get run over by a car on the way to visit your father—be careful!), or resonates with something we already know.

# The Scientific Interface

When you FOCUS on the experience you're about to have when you meet someone new, it alerts the hippocampus that this isn't just another run-of-the-mill moment in the day that can be tossed aside seconds after it occurs. By focusing first, you've already put the hippocampus on notice that the person you're about to meet and the name you're about to hear shouldn't be dumped on the daily scrap heap of disregarded experience. But the brain needs more than that to start setting up the neuron strings it requires to make a more lasting memory. As you've just been reading, the information that really sticks in the memory is the stuff that hits the brain several different ways, with each variation driving the memory a little deeper.

FOCUS can help, not just in giving the hippocampus a wake-up call, but in the energy and emotion you bring to focusing. When you FOCUS with a personal, emotional stake in meeting a stranger, the sound of the name and image of the face will claim lots more neuron strings than are set aside when you're sitting down to lunch and the waiter says, "I'm Brent and I'll be serving you today." But we want the info to be truly lodged in the memory, which means *using* the newly formed network of nerve cells. In its early stages, the network just hovers in existence, waiting to see if it's going to be put into action (in which case it'll stick around) or remain unused (adios!). That's why FACE specifies that you ASK to hear the name again, and ASK a few more questions—because you want to keep lighting up that brand-new neuron network devoted to the name of the person right in front of you.

The COMMENT step in FACE routes the name into the brain in yet another way. As mentioned above, the hippocampus is constantly sifting through new information for anything that jibes with what we already know. It helps if the COMMENT link is personal, but any connection to something you already know is useful, whether it's, "Harry—like my son's hero! All day, it's Harry Potter this, Harry Potter that . . ." or "Rick—I've liked that name ever since the first time I saw *Casablanca.*"

The final step in FACE calls on you to EMPLOY the name you've just learned. Saying, "Nice to meet you, Bill," is a hippocampus-friendly way of synthesizing the previous steps: you've FOCUSED on Bill, you've repeated his name when you ASKED about it, and you've COMMENTED on the experience of meeting him. The entire network of fresh neuron strings devoted to Bill are brought into play, which strengthens the network and increases the likelihood that his name and face will be easily called to mind when you run into him later that day in the elevator.

# Buttons, Lots of Buttons!

"Try to get as many possible touchstones as you can in memory storage," says Dr. Eric Kandel, founder of the Center for Neurobiology and Behavior at Columbia University in New York. " 'Deep processing' is the phrase that psychologists use for getting many associations between a given item or given name and memory storage," Dr. Kandel tells me. "The more associations you have with something the more likely you are to remember it, because it allows you to press a number of different buttons when you recall."

You'll add a brand new button when you've been using FACE for a while. A space will have been created in your memory for what, in effect, has become your hobby: collecting names and faces. Instead of a mind fascinated by the mating habits of tapirs, you'll have a preexisting neural network always ready to collect new names and faces. The hippocampus, after all, works overtime to assimilate new information that meshes with your personal interests. And because you'll be putting this interest in names and faces into the service of your career, for once that line from one of my favorite movies, *The Godfather,* won't hold true: when it comes to remembering names and faces, it's personal *and* it's business.

# CHAPTER 6

# Facing the World

Before moving on to the advanced level
of *Remember Every Name Every Time,*
take the FACE technique out for a spin.
Good luck!

"When I've just taken on a new assignment, I meet a lot of
new people, some of whom will work directly for me, some of
whom will be the next layer of reporting. It's important for me
to be able to identify them if I see them in the building—to say,
"Hi, Mary" or "Hi, John." That would be probably forty, fifty people, who could all be vital to the success of our company."

—*Brad Warner, Vice-Chairman, Fleet Boston Financial*

We've reached the end of Part One. *For many of you, mastering the
FACE technique will be all you'll ever need.* Throughout your career,
FACE will serve as a reliable tool to help you accomplish what previously seemed impossible: mingling at a business reception and remembering the first name of everyone you meet for the first time. Or
going into a conference room filled with strangers and walking out
with all their names easily accessible in your memory—for a short
while. With FACE, those new names will be handy all through the
event where you made the new acquaintances and probably into the
next day.

*That's usually sufficient to alleviate the terror so many people have
of meeting strangers at business and social functions.*

Getting the names and committing them to a longer-term memory is what I'll address in Part Two. I'll also address when, where and how you'll find it valuable to remember last names.

As you've discovered by reading this book, you don't *really* have a terrible memory for names. Your memory was simply undeveloped. Using the principles of FOCUS, ASK, COMMENT, EMPLOY, you'll find that you can develop a startling memory for names. But don't rush out to your company's next business-social function vowing to remember the name of *every* stranger you meet.

Here are some ideas for taking FACE out into the real world.

# Guarantee Success

One of the skills I've developed as a magician is juggling. It's something I taught myself and have since occasionally taught to people who sought me out as a coach. When I started working with beginners, the sessions didn't go as well as I had hoped. My students got discouraged quickly even though they went from being barely able to *hold* three balls at the same time to actually juggling them for a few seconds. That's because, in fairly short order, the balls always dropped.

This was frustrating for me, too. If I could juggle, I should be able to teach others. What could I do to make the sessions end on a positive note that would give my students something to build on, instead of inevitably ending in disappointment? I realized that I needed to *impose* success on the process. We would set juggling goals: using three balls, put them through the cycle three times. Then five times. Then ten times. Then stop—"See you next session!" My students would leave beaming at their progress—"I did it ten times!"—instead of hanging their heads and dwelling on the fact that they dropped the balls on the eleventh or twelfth go-round.

It was a big discovery for me: by setting and meeting reasonable goals, we have the ability to guarantee success (and, with it, the self-confidence and motivation to do more). We can then move on to establishing new, more ambitious goals. Initially, I just thought of this as a little trick I had learned about juggling instruction. Then I was talking to Charles Bronfman, co-chairman of the Seagram Company, and he mentioned a business concept he called "achievable units." Corporate planners have to be careful not to set impossible targets that guarantee "failure" even though great strides have been made, Charles told me. "It's important to work with achievable units as your goal."

I loved that phrase: Achievable units. It works, whether you're juggling three little red balls or the operations of a billion-dollar company. It also applies to memory training. Try to go into using the FACE technique with achievable units as your goal. Now that you're just about done with Part One of this book, put it down for a couple of weeks—unless you want to review the FACE chapter—and put the technique to work.

# The Out-of-Town Tryout

Don't take FACE to your next important business function intending to use it for the first time. Better to use the tack employed by Broadway producers: try out the show in other cities before taking it to the Great White Way. Try out FACE in settings where you don't have the added pressure of business concerns. There are countless events where you're going to meet strangers who don't have anything to do with your career but would make great FACE subjects. Fund-raisers for local organizations are invariably populated by close neighbors you know and others you're not so familiar with. If you have a child playing Little League baseball, ask yourself if you know the names of the parents of all the kids on the team. Maybe there's a dinner party coming up where you know the hosts but many of the guests will be new to you. Or there's a cocktail party on your calendar—now you won't have to wonder who'll be there or what you're going to talk about, because you've got something to do: try out FACE. What about a wedding reception? Go into it intending to get and remember the names of everyone seated at your table.

Remember: achievable units. Don't arrive at the next event swearing that you're going to remember the name of *every* person you meet. That's unrealistic. You probably already have a sense of what your capabilities were before you studied FACE. Set goals that are just beyond what you'd customarily accomplish. If you'd usually be a total washout at remembering names of strangers you met at a social event, tell yourself that you'll use FACE to come away with the names of two new acquaintances. If you know that you're already able to pick up one or two new names when socializing, set your sights on a higher achievable unit: four or five. *And don't raise your expectations until you've set a goal and achieved it a few times.*

Use FACE at four different nonbusiness occasions before you start using live ammo. By then, it would be great if you had established a goal of remembering six new names as your achievable unit. But if you just aren't there yet, don't worry. Work with what's comfortable—if coming away with two new names makes you feel a sense of accomplishment, build on that! Keep using FACE and more names will come with time. No matter how many new names you remember, as long as it's an improvement on your performance before you encountered this book, then you'll experience that heady feeling I like to call the FACE Lift.

## ONE MORE TIME!

**FOCUS**
> on this moment
> on this face
> on this person

**ASK**
> to confirm
> to spell
> for more detail

**COMMENT**
> to categorize
> to cross-reference
> to connect

**EMPLOY**
> while talking
> to educate others
> to end your conversation

## CATCH AND MATCH

I have a shorthand way of thinking about the FACE technique that I call "Catch and Match." Your first job in using FACE is to catch the name as it's being thrown in your direction (people innately sense that this is what they've got to do—hence the oft-heard phrase, "Sorry, I didn't catch your name"). That's what FOCUS and ASK are about—you're making dead-certain that you "see" the name coming your way and that you pull it in. In a football game, when a receiver runs a pass pattern and looks back to see the ball spiraling toward him, he has less than a second or two to identify the trajectory, estimate the speed and place his hands in the proper position just as the ball touches his fingertips. This is the equivalent of what you're doing when you FOCUS—you're totally concentrated on the task of catching the name that's coming your way. When you ASK about the name, you're like that receiver feeling the ball as it reaches his hands and pulling it in safely. But whether it's on the gridiron or in a conference room, just because you've made the catch doesn't mean you're done. Unless he's already scored a touchdown, the receiver has to keep on running. In our remember-the-name scenario, you need to follow the "catch" with "match" to make it a winner. And that means you'll need to work on the COMMENT portion of FACE—matching the name with others like it—in order to consistently get into the end zone.

Now close this book and try out the FACE technique in public. I'll see you in Part Two, where we'll move up to the next stage of remembering every name every time. In the meanwhile, have fun discovering exactly how good your "terrible" memory for names can be!

## PART TWO

# The Advanced Technique

# CHAPTER 7

# The NAME Technique: Nominate, Articulate, Morph, Entwine

### First you mastered FACE. Now step up to my advanced method of remembering names and faces—ten, twenty or a hundred at a time!

Here's Bob Elliott and Ray Goulding, from their classic comedy sketch, "Memory Expert."

> RAY: We pride ourselves on our interesting guests, and I think we have a great one here with us now. He's one of the world's most outstanding memory experts. His name is the Great . . . uh . . . the Great . . . uh, what was that again?
> BOB: My name is Hubert R. Gruber, Ray.
> RAY: Well, I thought you were known professionally as the Great something or other.
> BOB: No. I used to be billed as The Great Blotto, but I'm off the stuff now.
> RAY: I see. Well I know that many of our listeners will remember your act from vaudeville days, and I'm sure that they'd be interested in knowing, you know, what you're doing now.
> BOB: Well, I offer my services now to business and industry. I give courses in memory training to their young executives.
> RAY: That sounds like fascinating work.

BOB: You run across a lot of meatheads, but generally I can teach the young businessman to remember the names of people he's introduced to, and that's what's important.

RAY: Well, all right. Could you give us an example of how you do that?

BOB: Yes. Suppose you're introduced to a man named Fordyce.

RAY: Yeah.

BOB: Well, you form a mental picture of four dice and by always associating that image with the man, you never forget his name.

RAY: I see. Well, uh, how would that system work with me? My name is Goulding.

BOB: Well. Let's assume your name was Ramshot. You'd form a mental picture of a hunter shooting a ram. You'd remember the name that way.

RAY: What about my partner, Bob Elliott? How would it work with him?

BOB: Well, suppose his name was Richman. You'd form the image of a man surrounded by a lot of money.

RAY: In other words, pal, your system doesn't work with names like ours.

BOB: Well, yes it does. That's in the advanced training and I don't want to get into that on the air, Mr. Uh . . .

RAY: Goulding.

BOB: Yes. Goulding, yes . . .

I still get a kick out of that Bob and Ray routine. But I also find it a useful reminder of the kinds of mistaken approaches that others have taken toward memory improvement. The most obvious one is concentrating on remembering last names. Times have changed. When people say with exasperation after a business or social function, "I have such a terrible time remembering names," they're not talking about recalling the last names of their new acquaintances. Above all, they're focused on their first names. The measure of social intimacy is being on a "first-name basis." No one's goal is to be on a last-name basis.

# No Dice

Another priceless reminder from the Bob and Ray routine is the importance some memory experts place on techniques that are so simplistic they don't have any real-world value. Other than as fodder for a comedy routine, that is. If everyone had first names as vivid as Tiger Woods or Venus Williams, people wouldn't emerge from social events frustrated about not remembering names—we'd all be memory experts.

*The problem is that most names are not inherently memorable. Our challenge is to* impose *memorability on them.*

Another unhelpful tactic the so-called experts often recommend is to focus on some unforgettable facial feature—a wart, a red bulbous nose or a scar—and somehow link it to the person's name. *Walter*, say, has a conveniently prominent *wart*. Putting aside the question of how annoying you'd seem if you walked around parties focusing on people's physical imperfections, the basic problem is that most people simply don't have an unforgettable facial feature. Happily, we live and work in a world populated by largely unwarty, not-blotchy, scar-free humans. It's the *sameness* of faces, and *blandness* of most names, that test our memory. Tiger and Venus and Mr. Ramshot are the exceptions; two average-looking guys named John and Don wearing navy blue business suits are the norm (and the third guy in a suit probably *is* Norm).

# Memory-*Plus*

In the majority of cases when you want to remember folks you've just met, the FACE technique will be sufficient to ensure success. You'll have a vastly improved ability to remember the new names you encounter in business and social situations. But there may be occasions when you want to retain the information beyond the event.

Say you're in Bermuda for your company's annual weeklong off-site. On the first day you meet a newly hired but influential member of the marketing department. She's enthusiastic about a new project you've been developing, which is good news because she could prove instrumental in getting the project green-lighted. You're going to be running into this woman a lot at the off-site, and you don't want to be caught trying to sneak a peek at her business card every time you see her. You need to have her name fixed in your memory for several days, not to mention the weeks and months ahead.

Another scenario where you need additional memory-retention power is when you're meeting several people in quick succession—like in a conference room where you're making a presentation. What if you don't have time to use FACE thoroughly with each individual? That's precisely what happens to me every time I perform: I meet dozens and dozens and dozens of total strangers whose names I absolutely have to capture after exchanging a few pleasantries. If I fail to, I risk professional embarrassment in front of a large audience at the end of the show.

Whatever the reason for needing to supercharge your ability to remember names and faces, I've developed an advanced method to accomplish this called the NAME technique. As you remember, acronyms are unrivaled as learning aids. Well, you can't get a closer link between trying to remember a name and using a technique called NAME.

The FACE technique that you learned in Part One is designed to capitalize on the science behind the way memory works. FACE anchors a new name by using repetition, emotion, vocalization and a variety of other ways of activating the neuron strings that form memories. FACE separates the new name from the tens of thousands of other new pieces of information we encounter every day and instantly forget. NAME is very different from FACE in that it's a purely mental exercise—it does not depend on your steering a conversation toward the goal of remembering the other person's name. But NAME does share FACE's roots in memory science.

Let's briefly review that science. Everyone takes it for granted that some events are more memorable than others—the Hindenburg going up in flames, say, as opposed to a helium-filled balloon that a child has accidentally let go of at the zoo. But it wasn't until recently, with advances in neuroscience and the ability to observe the physical changes in the brain as memories are formed, that researchers began to understand *how* the brain sorts out which information to keep and which to discard.

According to these scientists, a region of the brain called the hippocampus filters our daily experience, picking out those items to be stored for later recall. The hippocampus is predisposed to select anything especially strange or vivid that it encounters, but also stays alert to new information that resonates with existing memories. But just getting a thumbs-up from the hippocampus doesn't ensure that anything more than a fleeting impression has been made. The new information has a much better chance of attaining memory status if it is processed or "encoded" by the brain in a variety of ways. If the bizarre or startling event is also linked in the mind to something familiar, and also recalled repeatedly, then a greater variety of neuron strings are called into play, making it easier to embed the new information in your memory.

Like the FACE technique, NAME utilizes what researchers know about the formation of memory, but comes at it from a different angle. As researchers are learning, mental functions tend to fall into "left brain" and "right brain" categories. The left brain handles language, logic and analysis, while the right brain is home to more artistic talents, such as imagination, color, music. Using the FACE technique is primarily what's called a "left-brain" activity: you're meeting someone new and essentially analyzing the person's name, cross-referencing it, examining it as a linguistic object (how do you spell Benjamin?).

The NAME technique calls the right brain into action, unleashing the imagination on any new name and face that you want to remember. It's a little more work than the FACE technique, but it creates stronger, longer lasting memories in two ways.

The first is that by using the NAME technique in conjunction with FACE, we gain more memory power than simply adding 1 + 1. Research has established that *when the left brain works in tandem with the right brain, the synthesis of analytic and imaginative skills results in an effectiveness level that's five to ten times what would be expected.*

The second way that NAME creates stronger, more enduring memories is that the technique capitalizes on the hippocampus's preference for new information that's extreme in a striking, weird or sensational way.

*We all have different thresholds for what strikes us as extreme, so feel free to tailor NAME to your own standards. But please be warned: I have a high tolerance for the surreal, so the imagery I suggest might not suit you. On the other hand, some people might think me too timid. In that case, indulge your imagination—and consider a career producing Hollywood action movies.*

Here are the four steps of NAME:

**NOMINATE,**
**ARTICULATE,**
**MORPH and**
**ENTWINE.**

## NOMINATE

While you're meeting someone for the first time and using the FACE technique, look at his or her face for a moment. Not an all-out stare, just a careful glance. Pick a feature, any feature. And I mean *any* feature. That's how the NAME process starts. If one aspect of the other person's face jumps out at you as especially memorable, like a woman's elaborately arched eyebrows or a man's handlebar mustache, then feel free to NOMINATE that feature—the way memorable movie performances are nominated for Academy Awards. But it doesn't matter if you choose another, much less striking feature, a run-of-the-mill nose or humble ear. What matters is that *you* surveyed the entire face and *you* made the selection.

Be careful about selecting anything that's subject to change. I sometimes choose eyeglasses, but be careful—people are always putting them on and taking them off. If you NOMINATE the glasses, the key to the whole NAME technique may be lost in someone's purse or pocket five minutes later. Pieces of jewelry, especially earrings, are also problematic—they're virtually guaranteed to be gone the next day. Even though I do it, I'm also wary of NOMINATING hairstyles, particularly women's hairstyles. Men tend to settle on one hairstyle when they're twenty-five and keep it more or less for the rest of their lives (if only I could have kept mine. . . . ). Women don't even have to get their hair cut to seem transformed; simply putting their hair up instead of wearing it down is sometimes sufficient to defeat NAME.

As to clothing—don't even think about it. Jackets can be removed midway through an event. Even the guy who looks like he lives in a charcoal suit will turn up on a casual Friday in a sweatshirt. When NOMINATING a person's physical characteristic, make sure you settle on something that's not likely to undergo a dramatic change in the near future.

Oh, and if you do NOMINATE a balding man's hairline, be careful. Sadly, I know that hairlines change dramatically over short periods of time. But NOMINATING them has its own particular drawback: men with receding hair hate it when you stare at their pate, even for a moment. You might be able to remember their names later, but they'll remember yours, too. And they won't be well inclined to you. Better to concentrate on features such as the eyes, nose, lips, ears, chin, eyebrows—even the overall shape of the person's head.

## ARTICULATE

I like to go dancing with my wife, Jenifer. In fact, we met on a dance floor. Unlikely as it may sound, that's the inspiration for the ARTICULATE stage in NAME. Actually, *learning* to dance was the inspiration. One piece of dance advice I've always remembered is: "If you can say it, you can do it." Unless you're a natural-born dancer, simply trying to copy an instructor's steps doesn't work nearly as effectively as first fixing the idea in your mind. *Saying* "step, cross behind, step, kick" actually makes *doing* it possible. I can vouch for that.

Having NOMINATED a physical characteristic of someone you've just met may not be enough to make the NOMINATED feature jump out at you when you encounter the person the next day, or week or month. Your attention needs to be fully concentrated, just for a moment, on that feature. And in that moment, silently ARTICULATE precisely what you observe. The person doesn't need to have Cindy Crawford's mole or Jay Leno's chin to elicit a detailed observation about the feature you've NOMINATED. Simply make a mental note about what you see: "Helen's eyes are blue-gray and ever so slightly bloodshot." Or "Ted's ear is pink and the lobe hugs his neck." Anything that comes to mind is of value, because what you're ARTICULATING isn't as important as the fact that you're devoting your undivided attention to the feature in question. Your brain is getting a message: *This is important—pay attention!*

You might find yourself protesting that you NOMINATED a nose, but a nose is a nose is a nose. It's not. Is the nose too large in proportion to the face? Does it tend slightly to the left or right? Are the nostrils prominent? Is the bridge rounded or flat? You could mention its color, its size, its shape. Or, after all this examination, you might conclude, "That's

**THE NAME TECHNIQUE**

the most normal-looking nose I've ever seen." Once you begin thinking about it, you'll find that there's always some observation that can be made.

The more you ARTICULATE, the better you'll get at it. The goal is to develop a useful mental vocabulary for describing faces. It may be a challenge at first because most of us aren't very articulate in describing faces. When, say, we're trying to direct a stranger to a friend in another room, we often resort to a description of their clothing: "He's the one in the red-striped tie" or "She's wearing a green dress." We're at a loss to precisely describe the way the person looks—which is fine, because the person we're talking to would probably be at a loss to apply a detailed description to the faces he sees. Do the best you can to ARTICULATE concerning the feature you've chosen—you're going to need it shortly.

## MORPH

Most names have no meaning, which is why they're so hard to remember. They don't correspond with a concrete word that can be easily pictured in the mind (unless they're in the special category reserved for the Tigers and Venuses of the world). Common first names are a closed circle of meaning. What's a Sam? What's a Susan? I'll grant you that "Don" can also mean putting on a hat, but that's not exactly a vivid image. Most names are simply random-seeming syllables, sounds that denote a name and connote nothing else.

That's trouble for your brain. The memory function is always striving to cross-reference new information with existing memories. Just adding "Sam" to the Sam file, with a whole new face attached, doesn't do much for its prospects of being remembered. But the great thing about names is they often sound similar to a word that's firmly rooted in the real world. "Sam," the vague three-letter phonetic cluster, sounds a lot like "Spam," a canned-food product that is a tad easier to conjure in your imagination. "Sam" also starts off the word "samurai." Which is easier to remember, the corporate VP with the nondescript name or a sword-wielding Japanese warrior?

The solution to the frustrating vagueness of names is to MORPH them into something that retains an element of the original but is much more graphic and will remind you of the actual word you're trying to remember. You can come up with your own MORPHS on the fly, or prememorize a list of the most common (and therefore most forgettable). You can find a list of these at the back of this book.

When you want to come up with your own MORPHS, or encounter a name that's not on my list, take care to choose a MORPH that will provide you with a solid visual image. I almost exclusively use objects for MORPHS because they're reliable image-generators. Nouns are far preferable to verbs and adjectives. MORPHING the name Sal into the adjective "salutary" isn't going to have a salutary effect on remembering his name. It's much harder to remember an idea than a thing. On the other hand, MORPHING Sal into a salami is much more promising. When I explain MORPH to my memory clients, I usually start off by MORPHING the name Tom into "Tommy gun." The violent implications of the machine-gun reference gets directly to the heart of NAME: we're going for maximum vividness here, in order to startle the brain into reacting with Full Memory Alert. But simply MORPHING a name into a word that carries a readily envisioned image isn't going to do anything to link that particular name with a particular face. To do that, we need to move on to:

## ENTWINE

I know you can kill comedy by overanalyzing it, but there's one other aspect of the Bob and Ray "Memory Expert" routine worth discussing. One of the reasons why Hubert R. Gruber's secret to remembering names is hilarious is that he so confidently touts half-cooked ideas. Though he understands that visual images facilitate memory, that's as far as he goes. He can only work with names that have obvious visual connotations. He's flummoxed by the name "Goulding" because he doesn't have a tool like MORPH to make it more manageable. Mr. Gruber also does absolutely nothing to connect "four dice" to Mr. Fordyce. There's no reason to think of four dice when you actually see the man's face.

Too bad Mr. Gruber didn't know about ENTWINING. That's where the NAME technique really gets interesting. You've NOMINATED a physical characteristic of the person you're meeting. You've ARTICU-LATED a mental description of that characteristic, fixing it in your brain as the target of your NAME exercise. And you've MORPHED the name into another word that immediately calls to mind a specific, clear image.

Now you've got two separate strands in play: a facial feature and a variation of the person's name. Here's the step that turns this stranger you've just met into someone whose name and face you're going to remember weeks, months or even years after a single encounter: EN-TWINE the two strands.

*The goal is to mesh the physical characteristic you've NOMINATED with the MORPH in a way that's unforgettable. And as an old-time memory expert once said, when you do this **the face will tell you the name.***

By ENTWINING, I don't mean simply picturing four dice next to Mr. Fordyce. Simple adjacency doesn't link the MORPH inextricably to the NOMINATED feature. You want to practically weave the two together.

How do you make that happen? The way to ENTWINE the characteristic you NOMINATED and the MORPH of the name is to put them together and create what I call "A NOVEL Color Picture."

Camera shops offer tips on how to compose better, more memorable photographs. They often suggest having your subject wear bright colors, getting the camera closer to your subject and trying to capture physical action, real emotions, or unusual settings. In other words, the secret to making more memorable photos is composing a novel color picture. It's also the secret of ENTWINING.

Before moving on to more details about "A NOVEL Color Picture," let's assume for the sake of this section of the chapter that you've just met someone named Bob. After looking over all his features, you've NOMINATED his nose. What MORPH would you choose? Bob, as in bouncing up and down in the ocean, or trying to grab an apple floating in a tub of water? Those aren't ideal—*verbs require too much work to visualize.* My MORPH for the name Bob is "bobsled." Picture a specific bobsled image—maybe the one used by the famous Jamaican bob-sled team? Once you've got an image fixed in your mind, we're ready to ENTWINE "bobsled" with Bob's nominated nose. Can we just picture it in place of his nose? While that's okay, we can do better. You don't have to use every element from the list below, but the more you do, the greater the effect.

Meet Bob. He can make your day—
or your month—if he purchases from
you instead of someone else.

Maximize your ability to ENTWINE with some or all of the six elements of:

**A**ctive

**N**ew
**O**bscene
**V**iolent
**E**xaggerated
**L**udicrous

. . . Color Picture.

- The "A" in "A NOVEL Color Picture" stands for Active, which is certainly appropriate for the bobsled. Imagine a tiny bobsled racing up, down and around Bob's nose as if it's the Olympic run at Lake Placid. *See* clouds of snow flying in the sled's wake.
- The "N" in "NOVEL" stands for New. Studies of how memory works indicate that when the mind is presented with a list of information, two entries in the list tend to make the strongest impression: the first and the last. The academic terms applied to this phenomenon are called the "primacy effect" and the "recency effect." In order to harness the power of the primacy effect, make it an important part of the ENTWINING process. The imagery you're conjuring is almost certainly going to be new, because—Jim Carrey aside—people don't tend to have Active events going on with their facial features when you meet them. They certainly don't have the decidedly new and unusual stuff you're going to be imagining—like the tiny bobsled roaring down Bob's nose. (Go for *new:* Simply imagining Sal with a salami next to his head doesn't qualify as utterly new, for instance, because we've all seen butcher shops where salamis are hanging near people's heads. In general, simply imagining an object *adjacent* to someone's face isn't "new," because that adjacency conceivably has occurred before. I'm talking about the really, truly *new*.)

**THE NAME TECHNIQUE**

- "O" is for Obscene. If you'd rather not rely on racy daydreams in order to remember someone's name, feel free to skip down to one of the other NOVEL choices. The initials in NOVEL are yours to choose from and can be used singly or in combinations. In defense of Obscene, I'd stress that we're only talking about the imagination here—seeing something in your mind doesn't mean you're endorsing it. It's not a case of having sexual thoughts about another person, it's having sexual thoughts about the person's *name*. The aim in NAME is to create an association with a name that is in some way startling, and it's okay if the association is shocking or even disturbing, because the sole purpose here is to *wake up the brain*.

Okay, now that the sermon's over, back to the sex!

In the bobsled scenario, maybe the sled is careening out of control because the man and woman riding in it have become so aroused by the excitement that they just can't wait until they get back to the ski chalet and are having sex right there in the bobsled as it hurtles down poor Bob's nose. As with all of these steps in ENTWINE, it's up to you exactly how graphic the image will be. For some, simply seeing the couple in the bobsled engaging in a deep French kiss will be obscene. Others might not be content until they're in NC-17 territory or beyond.

- The "V" in "NOVEL" stands, not surprisingly, for Violent. Again, this is a matter of taste. It's up to each individual to determine how mild or extreme the ENTWINING will be. I'm not *advocating* violence, of course. What I'm advocating is doing everything you can to help you become a master at remembering names and faces. Sometimes that may mean using a violent picture to bind the information to your memory. If you have a low tolerance for violent images, the bobsled scenario you imagine might not involve anything more than a wild ride on Bob's nose, with the sled shaking as it makes its run. But if you walked out of *Terminator II* saying, "What a bunch of wimps," no doubt you'll make the bobsled's adventures a tad more vivid. It may seem extreme to imagine the bobsled runners cutting Bob's nose, blood spurting at the bobsled's every turn—but I assure you that you're not readily going to forget the image.

- "E" is for Emotional—another NOVEL option that can be used, on its own or combined with another. We know that emotion makes anything more memorable, whether you're experiencing the emotion firsthand or witnessing it. In our bobsledding story, you might bring in your own joyful memories of sledding as a child. Or you can ascribe emotion to the characters involved in the story. The Obscene couple having sex in the bobsled could be having *great* sex. The driver of the tiny bobsled could be absolutely *ecstatic* with the thrill of his ride. Bob himself could be reacting emotionally to the action on his nose. He could be crying, cartoonishly squirting tears everywhere, at the Violent action he is being subjected to. He could be laughing uproariously from the New sensation of being tickled by teensy sled runners. Add Emotion to your ENTWINING and you won't risk ever feeling sad about forgetting a name.
- "L" rounds out NOVEL on a Ludicrous note. I know, I know: some smart aleck out there is thinking that a nose-carving bobsled is already pretty ludicrous. But not ludicrous enough! If you want to go this route with NOVEL, make the image *truly* ridiculous. The two most reliable ways to achieve complete ludicrousness are by imagining preposterous numbers of objects, or outrageous exaggerations of size.

Using the number approach, I might imagine tiny bobsleds shooting out of Bob's nostrils—not just a bobsled here and a bobsled there, but dozens and dozens of them, launched from somewhere deep in his sinuses.

Or you could go for the outsized option. Maybe the bobsled is a giant, ten-man behemoth—which Bob happens to be miraculously balancing on his nose like a performing seal with a ball. He staggers wildly around the room, desperately struggling to keep that bobsled balanced on his nose.

Whether we're talking dozens of nostril-clogging bobsleds or a wide load rig balanced on some poor guy's nose, it's all pretty Ludicrous, right? And dead certain to stick in your memory.

- It's important to remember that you're not just imagining A Picture, or A NOVEL Picture, but A NOVEL *Color* Picture. Bringing color to your fantasy is an essential part of the ENTWINING process. In our never-ending quest to activate as many different memory-forming neuron strings as possible, adding a specific color to the mix forces the brain to cross-reference the newly forming memory with its store of color memories. Is the bobsled featured in the Bob's Nose scenario painted red, white and blue for the U.S. Olympic team? Is it a sleek designer black? When the runners cut his nose in the Violent version, are his entire face and the front of his shirt red with blood? When Bob balances the huge bobsled on his nose in the Ludicrous version, does his face turn purple from the strain? I'd ask you more what-if questions, but I think you get the . . . Picture.

---

NAME stands for:
- Nominate—survey the face, then choose a feature, any feature!
- Articulate—describe the feature so you *know* it.
- Morph—names don't mean much, so transform 'em!
- Entwine—so that . . .

NOMINATED feature + MORPH = a lasting memory

---

### CATCH, MATCH AND ATTACH

In the FACE technique, we discussed another way of thinking about the process: as *catching* the name and *matching* it to someone else you know with the same name. In the NAME technique, it's a case of catch, match and *attach*. Instead of matching to an already familiar name, you're matching the name to an object that is your MORPH. Then you attach the MORPH to the NOMINATED feature.

You have the power to control your memory-forming ability. Create unforgettably vivid images in conjunction with a new name and face and you'll remember them like magic!

# CHAPTER 8

# Guess Who's Coming to Dinner

It's the classic Can You Remember
Their Names scenario: you, your spouse
or date, and six total strangers getting
to know each other over dinner.
Time to put NAME into action!

"I try to have a note with me that reminds me of who I'm
with—whether it's a new group of customers I'm entertaining, a
dinner party, or even a golf foursome—and then if I lose a name,
I can check."

—*Arthur F. Ryan, Chairman and CEO, Prudential Financial Inc.*

Circulating at a cocktail reception, you're on a hit-and-run, name-remembering guerrilla mission. You can almost pick your spots, falling into conversations where you want, with whom you want, and thus have lots of discretion about putting your memory for names to work. Not so at a dinner, where you're thrown into the company of half a dozen folks for an extended period of time. Unlike one-on-one meetings where it's a challenge to do the mental work of the NAME technique while simultaneously having a conversation, dinner parties are an ideal situation to try out your newly acquired NAME power. *At a dinner party, the faces you're studying are available longer than in a mingling cocktail crowd, and you're more likely to be able to focus on your fellow diners' features while they're eating or chatting with other tablemates.*

# The Appetizer

You've been invited to a dinner party that seems like an ideal chance to take NAME out for a test run. You're not on duty—clients won't be there, just folks from your industry along with their spouses. Most people hate to be the first to enter the room. They're missing a great opportunity. Be the first couple to get to the table. This gives you a chance to scan all the place cards of the people you'll be meeting. No faces to connect the names with yet, but reading the cards gives you a head start, tipping you off to the fact that there will be three Bobs showing up shortly, or a couple of guests with unusual names like Zelda or Ignacio.

Getting to the table before your tablemates arrive also ensures that you'll be likely to meet the other couples *as they arrive*. That's a lot better than being the last to reach the table (the worst-case scenario), which means you'll be playing catch-up with these strangers who've already introduced themselves to each other.

So there you are, ensconced at the table with your spouse or date. Another couple drifts over, finds the right place cards and sits down. After the initial hellos, the natural flow of conversation might be for your partner to speak with the person seated closest, and for you to speak with the other person. This gives you plenty of time to say, "Hey, I'm reading a book about remembering names. Please tell me about your name, Rob. It's short for Robert?" (You're beginning with FACE, laying the groundwork for NAME, which follows almost reflexively.) After a few moments, it's also natural for you and your partner to swap sides in the conversation; now you can focus on the other half of the couple you're meeting.

You're in good shape at this point, having spent some quality name-focused time with both people. Your small talk is about them—a good start. When the next couple arrives, it would probably be awkward to spend as much time talking about their names as you have with the first couple. That's too bad—but not a disaster by any means. Here's what you do: *introduce the first couple to the second couple.* By taking control of the situation and performing the introductions, you're essentially teaching the names of the couples to each other—which helps *you* remember their names. When the next couple arrives, you could play host *again*, but that might make it seem like you're trying to commandeer the whole table. You also risk getting tangled up by reciting too much new information all at once. You're better off simply keeping quiet and paying close attention as the new couple introduce themselves to everyone else. That way, when they finally get to you, you've already heard their names more than once and are well on your way to remembering them.

But suppose you were caught in traffic, or got lost on the way, or the babysitter showed up late, and you're lucky you got to the dinner at all. You scurry to your seats and there's a whirlwind of introductions that do you no good at all.

Ouch! Don't worry. First of all, let's alleviate some fears. These people might all be strangers, but presumably they're here to enjoy themselves. They're in a friendly mood and they're going to be even more well-disposed toward you when they see how well you remember their names! And you *will;* there's still time to assert enough control over the situation to ensure that you get the information you need. Throughout the dinner, make an effort to engage each person at the table in conversation. Start off by admitting that you didn't get the person's name as you were sitting down. I know it's counterintuitive for many business people to admit anything that would appear to put them at a disadvantage, but remember: *people almost invariably find it flattering that their name seems so important to someone else.*

You can use a condensed version of FACE here—FOCUS on the name and ASK to verify it. Across the table in a noisy restaurant or banquet room, there's probably lots of ASKING for verification that you can do. There won't be much time to make anything other than a brief COMMENT aloud (so double-up with your mental COMMENTS), but you'll probably be able to EMPLOY the name once or twice. Even if you don't get a chance to use FACE as thoroughly as you'd like, don't worry. You've got another trick up your sleeve: NAME, which forms an even stronger memory bond than FACE.

You've got another advantage. Before ever trying out NAME at a dinner party in real life, you had plenty of practice with the folks I've invited into this chapter and the chapters that follow. I've provided a blow-by-blow description of how I would use the NAME technique to get all of their names. To make these folks unforgettable, use NAME to come up with your own connections and images.

# Main Course

### LINDA

Meeting her, you start off with the usual FACE-informed banter. "Linda? Hi, Linda. I've always thought that was a beautiful name. It means something in Spanish, doesn't it?" And then you can introduce an innocuous, open-ended topic—"Tell me why you're here tonight." While she responds you can immediately move into NOMINATING a feature. I would almost always choose a woman's bangs if she wore her hair like this, but you could just as well select her nose or eyes, her lips or teeth or chin. Distinctiveness is great, but the important thing is surveying and nominating a feature, not the degree to which the feature itself is unusual or memorable. So, for me, the bangs.

Okay, Linda's bangs have won the nomination. What can you ARTICULATE about them? Well, they're not in a rigid line straight across her forehead. The hair sort of feathers to one side or the other, getting longer as it reaches the side of her face. The bangs don't hide her eyebrows; there's about an inch of space between them. Oh, and they're brownish-blond. There—the bangs have been ARTICULATED. Leonardo da Vinci wouldn't be proud, and the Mounties wouldn't be able to track her down—it's not a world-class description. But it doesn't have to be.

Now it's time to MORPH her name into something you can easily visualize. For the NAME technique, the name must be MORPHED into an object. In my experience, the name "Linda" MORPHS easily into "lint." It's a quick step to associate lint with Linda's bangs: We could imagine that once lint starts getting into her hair, extracting it is maddening.

That's how the process of ENTWINING begins: combining the feature you've nominated with the visual MORPH of the person's name. But simply visualizing some nondescript gray lint mixed in with Linda's nice blond bangs isn't nearly active and involved enough to achieve NAME's goal.

To make "lint" come alive for me, I searched my memory until I came up with some noteworthy fluff. The fuzzy gold sweater my wife wore when we were dating shed so much lint that we nicknamed it the Golden Fleece. Lint, to me, isn't just a kind of debris, it taps into specific, pleasant memories and thus becomes easier to remember as a MORPH.

But you don't have the Golden Fleece (lucky you), so you'll need something else to make lint more memorable. Imagine the lint in bunches of neon red and blue. Sometimes they get so entangled with each other that they dangle down from her bangs into her eyes, almost to her nose. This may be sufficiently vivid for some people, but not for everyone, and probably not if you're trying to remember many names for a long period of time. You'll have to take the image further. So: Linda starts trying to fight the lint epidemic, but for every piece she pulls out, a dozen more appear. It's like the chocolate-factory scene in *I Love Lucy,* when the assembly line keeps speeding up and Lucille Ball hilariously tries to keep up. In our scene, it's the lint production that's out of control, and Linda laughs at the unfolding comedy as she plucks faster and faster at her hair. She's laughing so hard that tears roll down her cheeks, which wets the lint in her hair, causing little rivers of red and blue dye to streak her cheeks, only heightening the comic effect. In the end, she gives up and allows the lint to keep multiplying until she's wearing a lint turban. Take a moment and make sure you really *see* this happening.

### TOM

Tom starts telling a story at the dinner table, and while he's talking it gives you a chance to work on his name. No offense, Tom, but you're not the most colorful-looking guy. That's okay—one of the main tenets of NAME is that you can NOMINATE *any* feature. It doesn't matter how remarkable it is. That's beside the point. The essential thing is that *you've* chosen it. In this case, I'll NOMINATE . . . Tom's ears. Once you've nominated a feature, start mentally riffing, or ARTICULATING, about it. Tom's ears, like so many, are pink. They're kind of shaped like a seashell (ditto). They might look like any other ears, but Tom's mother would always recognize them (well, maybe). There's no brilliant revelation here; the point is to engage your brain. I might even say to myself, "I nominate Tom's ears. His pink, close-to-the-head ears, which are classically proportioned and placed so that the top of the ear lines up with the eyes and the bottom lines up with the mouth."

You've concentrated on Tom's ears by NOMINATING them and ARTICULATING about them. Now it's time to go to Tom's name so it can be MORPHED into an image that can be ENTWINED with the nominated feature. I used to MORPH the name "Tom" into tom-tom drums, but I found that tom-toms didn't lend themselves to images vivid enough for my purposes. When you're trying to remember 120 names during a performance, you want images that would make Stephen King go pale. But if simply imagining Tom patting his ears like they were tom-toms is enough to burn the memory into your brain forever, that's great.

A more extreme tom-tom image would involve Tom smashing his ears like a percussionist running amok, with each blow making his ears bleed. But if we're going to get bloody, I'd prefer to use a MORPH that's more explicitly violent: the old gangster favorite, the Tommy gun. Does that mean I imagine the muzzle of a Thompson sub-machine gun sticking out of Tom's ears? Er, no. We're interested in violent, startling images here. When using NAME, you're directing an imaginary movie around you. If it suits you, you're the Sam Peckinpah or Quentin Tarantino of the business reception. So we need to have Tom's ears and a blazing Tommy gun somehow ENTWINED. Are the ears jammed into the trigger guards of two machine guns, spraying the room with bullets? Maybe. Or is someone else firing the gun and shooting off Tom's ears? I'd be most likely to go with the latter image, because seeing his ears popping off one at a time like toast springing out of a cartoon toaster is a picture my memory would find hard to shake off.

Of course, I'm not endorsing violence in any way. But I am endorsing vivid imagination as a tool to help you remember names and faces. You've gotten a comic and violent scenario here; now go ahead and picture it.

## SUE

Your spouse starts telling a story and you see Sue laughing and responding. Let's NOMINATE her lips, while noting (again) that any feature can serve this function. It's the fact that you choose the feature, and use it in the rest of NAME, that makes it memorable; the feature itself doesn't have to be strikingly unforgettable. If it is, it's a bonus. What can we ARTICULATE about Sue's lips? When she smiles, we can see a distinct bow shape. Focus on those lips. They're about to become very useful in remembering Sue's name.

But first, we've got to MORPH her name into something we can visualize in conjunction with her lips. Over the years, I've found that "Sioux" is a terrific MORPH for Sue. True, it's not an object, but it sounds exactly the same and comes with a wealth of imagery. Too much, in fact. Don't try to conjure up a fully-dressed Sioux Indian as an image. It's better to take one specific aspect of a concept and employ it as a MORPH. Sioux could be represented by a teepee, or a tomahawk, or an arrow. With Sioux/Sue, I picture a single arrow. As it happens, Sue's mouth has a *bow* shape. Bow . . . arrow. It's one of the rare occasions when the facial feature makes so much sense in combination with the MORPH that you may remember her name for the rest of your life. Don't look a gift MORPH in the . . . mouth. But it's such a rarity that I'm not going to pursue the whole bow-shooting-an-arrow scenario. Instead, let's go after a more likely way of ENTWINING the Sioux-arrow MORPH and her NOMINATED lips. The gentlest approach would have Sue pursing her lips and holding an arrow between them. If that works for you, fine. But I say, hey, it's just your imagination, why not go for broke?

Imagine the point of the arrow like a giant needle and thread, sewing her lips shut, with a single droplet of blood at the corner of her mouth. Yes, it's a kind of awful image, but I guarantee that it's more memorable than thinking, "How about Sue wearing a Sioux headdress?" There's nothing ENTWINED about wearing something *on* your head, and there's also nothing *new* about it.

It's my experience that the more extreme the ENTWINING, the more certain you'll be of remembering the name and face. So why not maximize your chances? I'm sorry if the image above shocked or disturbed you; my wife hates that kind of stuff. I find that throwing in a novelistic detail like a drop of blood makes the image much more memorable. But I understand if you'd rather use less over-the-top imagery.

*Choose what's comfortable—and* effective*—for you.*

Some of my clients have had great success with remembering women named Sue just by imagining their faces on the Susan B. Anthony coin, or as lawyers waving a summons and saying, "I'm going to sue you!" I'm leery of those memory strategies, though, because they don't inextricably link the name and face and aren't startling enough, or new enough, to ensure that they don't fade quickly. Besides, a subtler association like

the attorney suing requires you to insert lots of explanatory details. Violence is almost by definition quick and needs no explanation. It's my gut instinct that remembering names and faces is an extreme sport. Now that you've got Sue's story straight, visualize it.

### MICHAEL

You're going to meet a lot of Michaels in your life. That's good because it always presents you with the opening when using FACE to ASK, "You like Michael, not Mike?" It's also effective because, as with all more formal first names, I can immediately COMMENT, "Some people try to call me Ben, but my friends call me Benjamin." It's also a great name because there are so many famous Mikes and Michaels around (Michael Jordan, the New York Mets' Mike Piazza, computer guru Michael Dell, to name but three). That makes your mental COMMENT in FACE an easy task. I also love the name Mike because it MORPHS so easily into mike-as-in-microphone.

But I'm getting ahead of myself. First we have to NOMINATE a feature. The first thing I notice about this gentleman is his chin. What can we ARTICULATE about it? Mike's chin is strong, sort of oval, almost as wide as his mouth. Yes, you could say that about a lot of chins, but Mike's chin is the only one we're saying that about right now. Simply focusing on it makes his chin the center of our attention.

I've already mentioned my MORPH for Mike: mike. A microphone doesn't as obviously lend itself to action-packed imagery as a Tommy gun, but we can put it to work as we ENTWINE the MORPH (mike) and the feature we NOMINATED (his chin). Imagine Mike's chin itself as a microphone jutting out from under his mouth, as if he's a lounge singer who was involved in a once-in-a-lifetime accident. If I were having cocktails with Mike, with limited time—just seconds—this is as far as I could go. But since we've got a whole dinner to work with, I'd like to press home the point by showing how far you *could* go.

The image of Mike with the microphone chin still isn't as strong as I'd like because there's no action involved. Let's add some action and further ENTWINE these two! You need to make an announcement, so you grab Mike's chin and start speaking into it, and your voice comes booming out of his ears while his eyes, on springs, pop out of his head. He tries to push you away, but you hang on to the microphone chin and start singing into it, with your voice booming across the room. Finally, Mike shoves you away and the mike breaks off in your hand, leaving a mess of wires and metal where his chin once was.

Mike's going to have a heck of a time shaving that chin in the morning, just as you're going to have a heck of a time ever forgetting his name. Turn back to Mike's photo and picture it just for a moment.

## ANN

When you were just meeting this woman using the FACE technique, you learned that her name was Ann (in the ASK stage you found out that it was A-n-n, not A-n-n-e). Comments to yourself linked her in your memory to advice columnist Ann Landers, Henry VIII's second wife, Anne Boleyn and former Texas governor Ann Richards. But this is "ann" easy name to forget, you tell yourself, so you'll need NAME to make its position in your memory absolutely secure.

And the NOMINATION goes to . . . Ann's glasses. When she sat down at the table someone complimented her on her glasses and she made a joke about needing a guide dog without them. I think we can be pretty sure she won't be switching to contact lenses anytime soon. What can we ARTICULATE about the glasses? The frames are fairly thin, more cerebral than severe-looking. One of the arms is almost totally hidden under the sweep of Ann's hair.

Okay, we're halfway through NAME. The most obvious MORPH for "Ann" is "ant"—I've found it reliable dozens, if not hundreds, of times I've used it for my performances. Ants can be imagined busily doing something in relation to any feature you care to pick. In this case, they ENTWINE themselves with the feature of Ann's that we've NOMINATED, her glasses, by trooping across the tops of her frames, looping down along the bottom of the lenses and even skittering down the lenses themselves, holding on for dear life.

The image above may be enough for you great visualizers (or entomologists) out there, but in the interest of learning the NAME technique, let's go further. When Ann brushes away the ants, it only seems to spur more of them into action. Suddenly the glasses are swarming with ants, no longer the little black ants everybody knows, but now mixed in among them are bigger, fiery red ants. There are hundreds of them now, coating the front and back of her lenses, entirely blocking her vision, dripping off the tops of the frames. Ann takes her glasses off, sees that she's holding handfuls of these crawling insects and screams, dropping the glasses. They shatter on the floor, sending shards of glass and hundreds of ants flying everywhere.

Wait a minute, are we making a David Lynch film here or remembering Ann's name? This is probably enough ENTWINING—I think the pure creepiness of the image will give Ann a secure home in your memory. No need to escalate to *Attack of the Killer Ants*. But there's also no need to tame the imagery. Some of my clients try to ENTWINE "ant" with Ann simply by imagining a big ant sitting on her shoulder, but the passivity of that image makes it unlikely that they will still have her name, even a few hours after meeting her. There's nothing particularly antlike about sitting on someone's shoulder. You'd remember that there was supposed to be *something* on her shoulder, but what? A cat because her name is Cathy? A giant bee for Beatrice? No, it's crucial to include action—wild or bizarre action, whenever possible—to make the ENTWINING unforgettable.

### STEVE

When I use the FACE technique as I'm meeting someone named Steve, my first thought during the COMMENT stage is: Steve McGarrett of *Hawaii Five-0*. Someone else who made that connection might, in a variation on NAME, imagine our dining companion Steve wearing a Hawaiian hula skirt. Maybe a hula skirt is enough to trigger Hawaii → *Hawaii Five-0* → Steve McGarrett → Steve! But I doubt its ability to make the name last in your memory longer than the short time you're sitting at a table with him. I want Steve to stay with you out in the parking lot, in the elevator the next day, and maybe even when you run into him at the health club a month later.

Stick with the full NAME technique—trust me, as someone whose living depends on it, you're better off using every step rather than hoping the partial version works.

I NOMINATE the patch below Steve's lower lip, where (let's ARTICULATE) there's either no beard growing or the beard is very sparse. The lip sort of juts out over this space, throwing a little shadow. You might think: the space below his lip—what kind of feature is that? But I picked it because of its very vagueness, to demonstrate that *any* aspect of someone's face can be NOMINATED. It's what you *do* with the nomination that matters. But before we go there, we've got to MORPH Steve's name. You could use "sleeve," but that seems fairly limp. Invariably, my MORPH for Steve is "stove." Just as invariably, "stove" works, because it's just one vowel away from "Steve," and a stove presents lots of opportunities for memorable antics involving fire and smoke.

When I think of a stove, I think of the old-fashioned, pot-bellied, wood-burning variety, with a long stovepipe coming out of it. The way I'd ENTWINE the feature of Steve's face that has been nominated (the area below his bottom lip) and the MORPH of his name (stove), is to imagine a circular stovepipe poking right out from under his lip. His chin has turned into the stove itself. Under his beard, we can see the stove's grate, full of red glowing embers. The stovepipe perched above his chin belches clouds of white smoke and cinders, and the smoke turns his hair white. Most of the time, you don't have the opportunity to make up a long, involved story. More likely, you'll only have enough time to do what we've done with Steve: craft a simple, crisp and vivid image connecting "stove" to his chin.

That did it for me. How was it for you? Maybe you'd rather use a more modern stove in your fanciful vignette. Imagine the space below his lip as the burner on a gas range, which you turn on by twisting his ears. The more you twist, the higher the flame on the burner, which singes his nose. Whatever. It doesn't matter if your stove is for camping or for cooking in a restaurant. Just get the thing on Steve's face and make something happen. And be careful not to take Steve for granted. He *is* the last person in the series; but don't assume because his name is the freshest in your mind it will be the easiest to recall once some time has passed. Really focus on that stove image. It will pay off.

# Dessert

Now, without glancing back over the text of this chapter, look at the photos below and come up with the names of the six people you've just met. Use what you learned with the NAME technique!

What was messing up that blond woman's nice bangs?

Didn't the man next to her have some difficulty with his ears?

What was it about an arrow and the woman seated in the middle?

Why does the man seated to her left make me suddenly feel a song coming on?

Didn't the woman on the right need to call an exterminator for some reason?

The silver-haired gentleman makes me wonder: are they sitting in a smoking or nonsmoking section?

I trust that the ENTWINED images came quickly to mind, triggering your memory of each name (lint → Linda, Tommy gun → Tom, Sioux arrow → Sue, microphone → Michael, ants → Ann, stove → Steve). If you only got a few of the names right, or spent half an hour puzzling over the photo, I would urge you to reread both this chapter and the one in which the NAME technique is introduced.

If you got them all correct and are feeling sure of yourself, go back over the individual photos and switch around the things you've ARTICULATED. Instead of lint in Linda's bangs, ENTWINE the lint with her eyebrows. Instead of imagining a stovepipe lurking below Steve's lower lip, envision it sticking out of his right ear. Try this exercise with all six diners, and you'll see that—as I promised—*it doesn't matter which feature you select*, just so long as you select *something*.

Before you move on, here's one more little assignment: take a moment to *really* focus on the MORPHS for Michael, Tom and Steve:

- Microphone
- Tommy gun
- Stove

**GUESS WHO'S COMING TO DINNER**

In my career, these three names are among those I most often encounter. Having their MORPHS almost reflexively available is a huge help, as I suspect it will be for you. I hope that if you put this book aside and never read another page, you'll still have those three MORPHS locked into your memory for use with all the Mikes, Toms and Steves you'll meet in your business life.

But I also hope you don't put the book away right now, because the next two chapters are vital to making the NAME technique work with optimum effectiveness. In my experience with clients, I've discovered that almost nobody has trouble NOMINATING and ENTWINING. Conversely, some people have a hard time getting their heads around the concepts of ARTICULATING and MORPHING. I've dedicated chapters to both of those steps to make sure you get the most out of the NAME technique.

> • Try out (and practice) the NAME technique at dinners, where the usual two-second window of opportunity when meeting someone can easily turn into two minutes or even twenty.
> • You can *see* names that previously you could only *hear,* simply by:
> —changing the spelling slightly (Linda/lint, Ann/ant, Steve/stove)
> —finding a sound-alike (Sue/Sioux, Michael/mike)
> —augmenting the name (Tom/Tommygun)

> If you ENTWINE a name with a face, the face will *tell* you the name.

# **N A M E** in a Nutshell:

**N**ominate                    **A**rticulate

*A    Facial    Feature*

**+**

**M**orph

The name transformed into A NOVEL color picture

# Entwine

## The name transformed

# A Facial

Feature into A NOVEL color picture

# CHAPTER 9

# Unforgettable Faces

The first step to remembering faces—and
attaching names to them—is increasing your
awareness of faces in general. Here's how
to sharpen your natural ability to remember
every *face* every time.

"Last week, for the first time in my life, I met identical twins who are in business together. Both six-foot-one, both gray-haired. They are built the same way, they both dress the same way. It was unreal. I told them, 'The only way I can remember your names is by looking at your ties.' They changed ties on me yesterday, just to confuse me. It made me realize, when I meet an ordinary person who's got unique features how relatively easy it would be to remember the name. I realized that I've missed some real opportunities for remembering names."

—*Bob Marbut, Chairman and Co-CEO of Hearst Argyle Television*

From the moment we're born and begin taking in the most elemental information that shapes our understanding of the world, the human face occupies the most prominent place in our perceptions. Determining whether someone is a friend or foe just from looking at their face is an instinct that goes back to the dawn of our species. In fact, it appears that the memory for faces has its own special area of the brain. The evidence comes from a rare neurological disorder called prosopagnosia, which damages the patient's ability to recognize faces that had been familiar, yet leaves perfectly intact the ability to recognize everyday objects.

# You're Great at Faces— But You Can Be Even Better

Despite the special importance recognizing faces has for us, as we get older we start taking them for granted. Two eyes, a nose, a mouth— what's so memorable about that? Unusual faces still grab our attention, because they deviate from the prototypical face we've become accustomed to. But on the whole, we don't focus much detailed attention on the faces around us. Part of the reason is that we're so damned good at recognizing faces. Most of us aren't great at verbalizing what we perceive about faces, but we rarely confuse one person for another. There might be two thirty-four-year-old guys with almost identical ethnic backgrounds working down the hall, neither with any distinctive features, but once you've gotten to know them you're not going to mix them up.

I remember reading once about a study that involved showing 1,000 slides of faces to a group of people, then showing the same slides to them again, only with 100 new faces sprinkled throughout them. A startling percentage of the test group immediately noticed whenever one of the newly added faces popped up on-screen. The test group hadn't been instructed to make any special effort to memorize the faces of the original 1,000. Just seeing the faces made them infinitely more memorable than if the group had only heard the names of the people shown in the slides. Imagine hearing 1,000 names read aloud, and then hearing them again, with 100 new names added to the mix. I'd be shocked if most people could pick out a dozen of the new names. Visual information of *any* kind is more memorable than information we hear—that's why people under hypnosis are able to recall images like license plate numbers that they couldn't consciously bring to mind. It's also why we find ourselves saying, "I know your face, but I can't remember your name," and not saying, "I know your name, but can't remember your face."

Faces are always our prompts to remember someone's name. The reason why the prompts sometimes fail us is that we're so casual about faces—they're easy to remember, so why devote much attention to them? Because faces are crucial to remembering names; you can't just wing it when looking at faces. You need to heighten your awareness of faces, learning more about facial features so that you'll be able to absorb more information about faces—and thus the names that are attached to them. Developing your skill in this department will be a tremendous help in using the NAME technique. Once you know more about faces and have a heightened interest in them, you'll have a lot more to say when you ARTICULATE.

# Just Browsing

I had to become more aware of people's faces after I made remembering names a crucial part of my performances. On many nights, I was working for a crowd of more than 100 white males, between 40 and 60 years of age, with similar haircuts, blue suits and the same lack of facial hair. I'd walk into the room and want to scream *help!* I quickly developed an intense fascination with the nuances of facial characteristics—it was the only way I'd be able to remember the names of those folks. In this chapter, I'd like to pass along some of the insights I've gained so that you'll be as effective as possible in ARTICULATING about faces, and therefore better at using the NAME technique.

A turning point for me was reading a book called *Amazing Face Reading: An Illustrated Encyclopedia for Reading Faces,* by Mac Fulfer. He's a lawyer who became fascinated by the science of "reading" faces, called physiognomy, when he decided to learn more about faces in the hope that this skill would help him during jury selection.

I'm not so sure about his conclusions regarding the link between personality types and their facial profiles, but parts of the book were fascinating. Here's a guy who devotes four pages to eyebrows! I had never even really thought about eyebrows before, only vaguely noticing them if they seemed particularly striking—as when Brooke Shields became famous. Now I was reading about bushy, thin, winged, chameleon, high, low and tangled eyebrows. The more I became aware of eyebrows, the more interested in them I became, and the more attention I paid to them when meeting people. The more attention I paid, the stronger the reaction of my mind in making memory space available for all this new information.

When you're reading a magazine, standing in line at the movie theater or in an airport, spending any time at all where you can study other people's faces, really look at their eyebrows. Are they high, with a considerable space between them and the eyes, or are they low, seeming to sit on the eyelid? Do the women you see pluck theirs and then pencil in a line, like movie stars of yore, or do they let their brows grow naturally? Are the brows you see the same color as the person's hair, or lighter, or darker? Is there a wide space between the eyebrows, or are they so close together that they seem to be almost one continuous line? Once you start focusing on a facial feature, it's almost hard *not* to keep noticing it everywhere you go and to compare all the new examples you encounter in the course of a day. But don't just focus on eyebrows. Make it a game—this week, I'm checking out eyebrows, next week, I'm on nose patrol. Every week for a month or so, select a different facial feature and for those seven days make that feature your hobby.

# Get a Vocabulary

It's vital to develop a vocabulary for ARTICULATING facial features. The process of learning more about faces and as a result becoming more aware of them reminds me of when I was a young man and first noticed women's perfume. I'd go out on a date and report back to a pal that "she smelled great," but I couldn't be any more specific than that. Perfume was perfume, I thought, though I could tell that the scent a young woman I was going out with didn't smell anything like my Aunt Polly's. Then one day, killing time in a doctor's office waiting room, I came across an article in a women's magazine that talked about the four basic perfume aromas: citrusy, spicy, floral and musky. From that day on, whenever I've gotten a whiff of perfume, whether it's something new my wife is wearing or a scent wafting through the elevator, I can have more to say to myself than an inarticulate "Mmm!" or "Yech!"

I'm not an expert, but at least now I have a basic vocabulary to work with, which goes to show that the more you know, the more you can describe. A great source of knowledge about faces is the quarter century of research into facial biometrics performed by scientists seeking to develop face-recognition technology for personal identification. The goal is to make PIN numbers and passwords obsolete, as computers simply read and identify individual faces. That may still be a ways off, but the research has yielded lots of fascinating information about faces. For instance, there's the concept of "eigenfaces," or primary faces. By collecting and combining a large number of faces in a database, researchers have come up with a set of eigenfaces—two-dimensional masklike images of light and dark areas. The eigenfaces are the result of amassing all the photos and then identifying what groups of individual faces have most in common, and where they differ the most.

If you're having a hard time ARTICULATING anything about the feature you've NOMINATED, it might help to do a restart of the process, surveying the face the way a computer does, paying attention only to light and dark contrasts. Using the eigenface approach, you might suddenly notice deep eye sockets or hollow cheeks and find yourself ARTICULATING almost simultaneously with NOMINATING—when only seconds earlier, you thought you had nothing to say.

# Call the Cops!

Eigenfaces are impressive science, and I'm sure we'll all be astonished when the ATM machine obeys our commands after just one glance at our face. But it's really just a digitally souped-up version of what police artists have known for decades. The police artist's goal is to use information furnished by witnesses to create a portrait that looks as much as possible like an individual person, not a generic image. Their primary focus, at the start of the process, is to establish the shape of the suspect's head.

Police artist Douglas P. Hinkle published a book called *Mug Shots* in 1990 that laid out the principles of his profession. He described the most common head shapes (the top four are narrow oval, oval, moon-shaped, heart-shaped—bet you didn't know that, just as I didn't know the four basic perfume varieties). Even though the shape of a head isn't technically a "feature," sometimes I NOMINATE a head shape when using the NAME technique. Nobody's going to have a perfectly oval head, but some people come pretty close—which is fine for NOMINAT-ING and ARTICULATING purposes.

For years, I never understood what people meant when they said something like, "So-and-so has a high forehead." I always thought: "Compared to *what?*" Then I read Hinkle's description of how, after es-tablishing a suspect's head shape, police sketch artists move on to defining the distances between features (hairline to eyebrows, inside corner of one eye to inside corner of the other, bottom of the nose to the top of the upper lip). The usual distance between the eyebrow and hair-line should be the same as the distance from the hairline to the top of the head. Deviations from that standard make a face notable, either for having a high forehead or a low one. He also talks about using the length of one eye, corner to corner, as a good unit of measurement for the face. Eyes are usually separated by the length of one eye. It doesn't take much deviation from that measure to make someone look dramatically different, whether the eyes are closer together or farther apart.

You'll find the same sort of obsession with the relationship between facial features in drawing classes. Students learning to draw the human face first learn about the standard distances between features, so that they will note how features vary from individual to individual. Faces are usually "five eyes" wide. The distance from the bottom of the eye to the top of the eyebrow is usually one eye width. From the bottom of the lower lip to the tip of the chin is also one eye width. From the top outside of the nostril to the middle of the eye? You guessed it—one eye width. *Once again, any deviation from these standards makes the face remark-able.*

# Don't Be Embarrassed. Go Ahead, Look

I know some readers will worry that if they're always staring at people's faces, someone's going to take offense. That's true if you're sitting on a bus fixated by the nose of the person sitting across from you. But don't worry about somehow putting off people during conversations. The other person won't know that you're looking at his or her face with the attentiveness of a plastic surgeon sizing up a new patient; *your focus will only seem like a flattering display of interest.* I recall reading about a psychological study of two groups of people; one group was instructed to have a regular conversation with another person, the other coached to count the number of times the other person blinked during the conversation. Afterward, the researchers talked to the people who had been on the other sides of the conversations and discovered that they felt much more positive about their interactions with the blink-counters. Even if you're only counting blinks or studying the amount of space between the tip of their nose and upper lip, seeming to pay close attention to the other person inspires a better reaction than if you're just shooting the breeze.

# Does She Need a Nose Job, or Is She a Spy?

That line in the previous paragraph about imitating a plastic surgeon looking at a new patient wasn't too far off the mark. I want you to bring that degree of focus to looking at people's faces. You can assume any number of mind-sets when looking at faces. A great way to acquire new information is to assume a new role. Different jobs have different interests and, as a result, pursue different lines of inquiry. As a plastic surgeon, you might examine faces with the intention of finding what you'd change if you could—flatten the nose a bit, unwrinkle the forehead, build up the chin? Or pretend you're an optometrist. Is that woman wearing contact lenses? *Precisely* what color are her eyes—are there any flecks of gold among the green? Maybe you're a spy, and the woman you're talking to is a double-agent who has a microdot hidden somewhere under the skin on her face—look at every inch of the surface for the slightest bump.

There are a couple of ways to really examine a face. One is to look at it and mentally draw the letter Z across it: start at the eyes and eyebrows on the left, zip across to the right, down diagonally across the nose, then left to right across the mouth. Another is to draw a figure eight, circling down from the eyes to the mouth and back up again. Little drills like this help to ensure that you're really taking in the whole face, rather than just noticing eyes that are more widely spaced than usual and then leaving it at that.

In the course of your face investigations, try not to limit them to homogeneous groups. If you always practice on TV news anchors, you're not going to get a very wide sample of facial features, because newsreaders are chosen for those jobs precisely because of their standard-issue appearance. Developing an ability to discern subtle differences in a homogeneous group like that is one way of sharpening your skills, but an easier way at first is to cast a wider net, studying faces of people from all walks of life and every ethnicity. You'll develop a greater vocabulary for thinking about faces and describing them. And, given the riotous mix of features, complexions and expressions in the world, I guarantee that you'll never get bored.

---

- Don't be afraid to look.
- Look through new eyes—a plastic surgeon's, an optometrist's, a photographer's, a sculptor's.
- Practice ARTICULATING using the faces you see in magazines. Try to give one descriptive line about every face you see in today's newspaper. Mentally ARTICULATE about the faces you see while waiting in line at the bank, the movie theater, in an airport.

---

More interest in faces = a better chance of remembering them.

# CHAPTER 10

# Naming Names

What's in a name? A handful of letters,
a sound or two—and not much more.
At least on the surface. Focus closer on
names—discover their origins, juggle them
with wordplay, learn to make MORPHS—
and you'll find a fascinating new world.
It's a vital step in conditioning your memory
for optimum use of the NAME technique.

"I learned over the years, when I was less confident of myself,
that I would be so focused on introducing myself properly to
someone that I literally wasn't paying attention to their name. I
think a lot of people get into that trap. You're hearing but not lis-
tening. I have gotten over that—I listen, and I've got the name in
the moment. The question is: Can I remember it later?"

—*Mike Zisman, Executive Vice President for Strategy of IBM's
Lotus Development Corp.*

If we can substitute a strongly visual, somewhat similar word to
serve as a symbol for a name, recalling that name becomes infinitely
easier. That's because MORPHS enable you to see something you'd
normally only hear. Remember the MORPH and you're 90 percent of
the way to recalling the name.

There's a strong precedent for this in the world of, of all places, competitive Scrabble players. The National Scrabble Association has compiled a list of ninety-six two-letter words acceptable within the rules of the game. Just memorizing these few words, says the N.S.A., will add thirty or forty points to a player's score. It's a simple but inspired way of strengthening your abilities. MORPHING names is a similarly surefire way to radically improve your memory for names.

The parallel extends even further. The N.S.A.'s ninety-six words fall into three basic categories: words you already know; words you need to be made aware of; words you need to learn. MORPHS are like that as well. The N.S.A. points out that there are some obvious two-letter words such as "we," "be" and "up." Well, there are some names that are "obvious" and don't require much work, names like Fern, Rose and Frank. Then there are the N.S.A.'s two-letter words that, once you think about them for a second, make sense: "Hi," "ab" (as in abdominal) and even the musical scale "Do," "Re," "Mi," "Fa" etc. Those are kind of like names that we can push for real-world meaning: John, like toilet; Bill, like a duck's bill; Jack, like the gadget in your car trunk.

And then there are the two-letter N.S.A. words that are so far out in left field that you've got to familiarize yourself with them first before you can learn them, words such as "aa" (rough, cindery lava), "xu" (the Vietnamese monetary unit), and "ai" (a three-toed sloth). Those are the equivalents of names that require us to *impose* meaning on them: Kevin MORPHS into "cave-in"; Eric turns into "ear ache"; Larry into "lariat."

# Making Morphs

But how do we construct an effective MORPH? How can we convert a name like Bob, which doesn't have much to distinguish itself (sorry, all you Bobs out there), into something unforgettable? By MORPHING it into a word that is close enough to "Bob" so that their linkage is clear, yet is utterly different. The MORPH then packs all the meaning and substance that poor old Bob lacks. What does the name you're trying to remember sound like? Bob can lead us to "bobsled," which is a tad easier to remember—screaming down a mountainside, ice shavings flying—than blah Bob. Keith sounds like "keys"—not as action-packed as bobsled, but still a substantial, memorable *thing*.

MORPHS come from a variety of sources, dictated by the nature of the names being used. Some names, like Bill, also exist as English nouns that immediately conjure concrete images. Other names, like our friend Bob, are also English words, but they're most commonly used as verbs (as in: to bob for apples), and have to be tweaked into noun forms (bobsled). Often the name doesn't also exist as a lower-case English word, but the addition of a word immediately brings to mind a familiar image: Scott, with the addition of "towels," is easily *absorbed* by the mind. Another tack is to change a letter or two in the name to transform it: substituting an "I" for an "L" in Allen gives you an alien—the next time you see Allen but imagine him as an ET-like alien, you won't need to phone home to find out what his name is. Once you've got the eye-catching, memorable images spawned by the name, you're ready to put it into action with the ENTWINE stage of the NAME technique.

# Want to Get Better with Names? Get Better with Words

MORPHS will also flow from the personal history, background and associations that you bring to making them. The more general interest you have in names themselves, and even in words and wordplay, the more you'll be able to maximize the benefits of MORPHING (and the more you'll bring to the COMMENT stage of the FACE technique as well).

Familiarizing yourself with name derivations will help to make many names mean more to you, giving your memory a boost in its efforts to recall the name. Throughout my school years, I'd hear the name "Charlemagne" in discussions of French history, but the name never meant anything more than that to me until Jenifer and I began looking into names before the birth of our first child. Then I discovered that "Charlemagne" simply means Charles the Great—or magnificent, in effect. (Tempting, but we chose "Nathaniel" instead.) I had never put "Charlemagne" in my mental cross-referencing file for the name "Charles," but you can bet the medieval ruler flashes through my mind whenever I hear that name today.

But beyond simple fun, wordplay helps to keep your mind nimble and alive to new ways of looking at language. When the wordplay also involves names, it creates countless new threads of memory-aiding cross-references that will ultimately help you to remember names.

Several top executives I know regularly do crossword puzzles as an intellectual exercise to keep their minds sharp. An added benefit is that crossword puzzlers already have a head start on the rest of us in working with unusual names because they regularly find themselves penciling in Peruvian singer "Yma Sumac," actress "Una Merkel" and Italian actor "Ugo Tognazzi."

Anagrams are another variety of mental recreation that can give you a jolt of cerebral fun, which helps spark the mind and the memory. The name "Gary Gray" sounds bland and, well, gray, until you realize that his first name is an anagram of his last. An amusing nugget of info—and it means your mind likely will always have a strand of memory to make you think of the anagram whenever you see the name "Gary." The same goes for "Ronald Arnold" and "Lionel O'Neill." Whenever I see the first names "Ronald" and "Lionel," I instantly think of their potential anagrammatical last names.

Palindromes involving names practically provide their own MORPH-ING material. I get such a kick out of the backward-forward spelling of "So, Ida, adios" that when I actually met an Ida one time, I almost said good-bye before hello was out of my mouth. "Tis Ivan on a visit" is so evocative that if I even read the name "Ivan," I instantly see a burly man in fur hat pounding on my front door. And then there's the palindrome we all learned as kids, "Madam, I'm Adam."

Here's an assignment for you wordsmiths out there: compose a palindrome using names that are themselves palindromes, such as Otto, Bob and Hannah.

# Gorgeous George

The MORPH you choose doesn't have to be a sound-alike, it just has to be so closely linked to the target name that one almost reflexively follows the other. Donald might MORPH into duck. A name like George can go either way: the yawning chasm of a gorge, or George Washington, symbolized by a powdered wig or wooden teeth.

Commonly occurring names usually consist of just one or two sylla-bles—Linda, Mike, Sue, Bill—and that simplifies matters for MORPH-ING purposes. But MORPHING can certainly handle multisyllabic names. For instance, I prefer to be called the triple-syllable Benjamin rather than plain old Ben. If you were MORPHING Ben, you might choose a bearish image from *Gentle Ben,* or perhaps the London land-mark Big Ben. To get the full name, you've got two choices. The first is either to select a name like Benjamin Franklin and MORPH an image associated with him—the pot-bellied stove he invented, for instance, or a lightning-attracting kite. Or you can MORPH all three syllables. A couple of possibilities: Bench-a-man (a football player being shoved down into his seat) or Bendy-man (like the rubbery Gumby character). Other MORPHS I've come up with over the years: Bench (Idi) Amin; A Bun Jammin'; Binge, Amen. I like Binge, Amen, but that requires vi-sualizing a lot of information. You've got to think about bingeing *and* thanking God. A single object is best. But be careful about choosing an object that's indistinct. A hundred-dollar bill might serve for Benjamin Franklin, but it's still just a piece of paper and, in your memory, could look an awful lot like a ten-dollar bill.

# Harvesting a Christmas-Tree Forest

Not that the MORPH has to be an excessively precise match. I use a Christmas tree to MORPH Chris, Kris, Christine, Christie, Kristy and Christopher. The MORPH just has to get you in the right neighbor-hood for the name; once you're there, your natural memory will direct you to the correct address. The only exception to this is when the name you're trying to remember is completely foreign to you and each sylla-ble has to be recalled precisely (see Chapter 12, "Challenging Names, Challenging Faces"). And don't be afraid to drop a MORPH if it's not working, and come up with a better one. I used to think that the name Charles sounded sufficiently like "marbles" that I used the latter as a Charles MORPH. But as soon as I was once nearly stumped trying to remember a Charles's name and nearly went crazy before finally recalling it, I lost my marbles and switched to another MORPH: "chars."

The "chars" MORPH has the advantage of beginning with the same first letters as the name I'm trying to remember, and offers the chance for some sooty fun when it comes time to ENTWINE the MORPH using the NAME technique. (I tried for a while to use Prince Charles as a MORPH, with a crown as the symbol for his name, but dropped it when I found the crown jumbling up with a slew of Elizabeths, Victorias, Georges, Richards and other famously royal names.)

# The Ultimate Morph Crib Sheet

*MORPHS don't last forever. They remain in place in your memory as long as you need them to help you to get over the recognition hump. Once the name and face you'd like to recall have moved into your long-term memory, once you've* learned *the name, the MORPH will fade away.*

In the meantime, have fun coming up with your own MORPHS. But you don't have to reinvent the wheel. I've been creating MORPHS for years, and road-testing them to make sure they work efficiently. I've put together a chart of America's 40 most common men's names and 40 most common women's for people between 25 and 60 years of age—in other words, the people you're most likely to meet on the job.

It's worth noting that MORPHS for common names are extremely valuable because run-of-the-mill names are not only difficult to remember because they lack novelty, they're a challenge to remember using the FACE technique—getting into a whole conversation with someone named Arturo about his name is a heck of a lot easier than it is to chat with Bob about his name. Luckily, just when FACE's effectiveness is most challenged, the NAME technique steps in. If you do nothing but learn the top ten MORPHS on each list, you will have made your life much, much easier. If you familiarize yourself with the entire MORPH list, you're practically a pro.

The name-and-MORPH table begins on page 214. Learning it will require a little work at the outset, but you'll find these MORPH "short-cuts" are powerful tools to assist your growing memory skills.

To make effective MORPHS:
- Begin with the same letter of the name you're MORPHING.
- Try to choose sound-alike *objects,* rather than verbs or adjectives.
- Choose distinctive objects (beware the hundred-dollar bill vs. ten-dollar bill trap).
- When necessary, you can make an effective MORPH by using an image inspired by the name, whether it's Benjamin (Franklin)'s kite, Judy (Garland)'s ruby slippers or the shovel that leads you to "Doug."
- Be imaginative—what does the name *sound* like?
- If the name seems overwhelming, break it down into one-syllable components.

- MORPHS enable you to *see* names that normally you only *hear.*
- More interest in names = a better chance of remembering them.

# CHAPTER 11

# The Conference Room Challenge

You're about to walk into a conference room, intent on impressing six strangers. Fancy charts and a laptop-driven slide show would be nice, but you'll maximize your chances of a rave review by remembering those half-dozen new names.

"Depending on the nature of the meeting, I will take business cards and align them in relation to the people sitting around the conference table. Or I will take out a blank sheet of paper and write down people's names, creating a seating chart. What ends up happening is I tend to spend less energy on actually remembering the person's name—so when the meeting's over and people move around, I'm in worse shape than I would have been without that crutch."

—*Doug Braunstein, Head of Mergers and Acquisitions, J.P. Morgan*

A few chapters back, I introduced you to the NAME technique and followed it up with a sort of workbook chapter that let you try out NAME on the guests seated at your table for a dinner party. I chose that setting for the first photo-testing of your NAME mastery because real-life dinner parties are great places to try out the technique. They're a much better proving ground than a one-on-one encounter, where you're obliged to hold up your end of the conversation. The people whose names you're remembering using the NOMINATE, ARTICULATE, MORPH and ENTWINE method are sitting ducks at the dinner table. They're likely to be engaged in conversations with others around them and probably oblivious to the fact that one of their tablemates might appear to be focused a tad intently on the facial features of the other diners. (We're not talking stalker-quality staring here. It's just a matter of twenty seconds or so once you're adept at doing the four step NAME process.)

Implementing NAME while in a group takes the pressure off; the other people provide their own distractions while you're doing your memory work. And nobody will notice if you happen to use some people's names—because you've remembered them—but not others. Working in a small group of people is a step closer to the challenge of one-on-one, but not that far removed from simply trying NAME out on folks you see on TV or in a magazine.

Let's put NAME into action in a different setting: the conference room. You're more on the spot than at a dinner function—no plateful of pasta to hide behind while processing information. Like in a one-on-one setting, you'll have to hold up your end of the conversation in a business meeting. But your end is going to be a lot smaller in the conference room, since several other people are involved in the discussion.

I don't mean to make conference room meetings with strangers like the ones pictured here sound like a cakewalk. Some of my clients have told me it's their nightmare scenario, and it can be terrifying: walking into enemy territory and being machine-gunned with half a dozen names all at once. The NAME technique is crucial to handling the conference room challenge, but there are a few preliminary steps you can take to make the task of meeting these strangers less daunting.

Even I can't cope when someone rattles off a series of names and only indicates whom the names belong to with a cursory wave of the hand. The first step is to *take control* of the introductions. A good-natured laugh, accompanied by "Whoa, that went by too quickly for me!" will allow you to reset the process and convey the message that you care

about being accurate and thorough—while also emphasizing that these names and these people matter to you. Or you can hijack the process right from the beginning; when your host says, "Let me introduce everyone," pleasantly but emphatically reply, "That's all right, I'd like to meet them one at a time." Even if you knew in advance the names of the people you're meeting, when they're hurled at you all at once it's almost impossible to correctly attach the names to their respective faces.

Once you've put the brakes on, everyone will see that you're going to take your time meeting them. They'll return to their conversations until you get to them. Another tack is simply to ask for business cards. If the setting allows it, read the name out loud from each card (the EMPLOY stage of FACE) and shake hands with each person, introducing yourself as you go along. Once you're seated, arrange the business cards in front of you to reflect the seating arrangement. (The other features of FACE, by the way, aren't going to be as much help here because the conference-room scenario probably precludes taking the time to FOCUS, ASK, COMMENT and EMPLOY with each person you're meeting.)

You can *really* take control of the introductions by arriving early for the meeting. Getting the names of your conference-room *confreres* would be infinitely easier if you met them one at a time as they arrived for the meeting. Imagine how much more relaxed you'd be if you walked into the room and there was just one person to meet, like Mary from Human Resources shown here instead of the Gang of Six shown on page 141.

Previewing is another way to improve your chances of remembering the names of everyone in a group-meeting situation. If you arrive early and there are place cards on the table, study who's sitting where. Donald Marron, chairman, Paine Webber, says that he reviews lists of the names of people he'll be meeting with—even though he doesn't consciously make an effort to memorize the names on the lists. It's important to have the names of others in mind because "the securities industry is very heavily a people business," Don tells me. "We don't make anything, we don't have manufacturing plants. Our business is relationships. Remembering names is such an important part of communicating with people and interacting with them."

Previewing will help to foster an atmosphere where you're more likely to remember the names of everyone in a conference-room meeting. But the only surefire way of going into a group meeting with strangers, using all their names confidently in the meeting and emerging with those names locked away in your memory is by using the NAME technique.

I can't accompany you on your next foray into a conference room, but I have devised a photo-drill for this chapter that will help you to practice navigating through meetings successfully. Here goes:

You've just been hired for a high-level job by Murphy's Manufacturing Corporation. You'll be the CFO's direct report, a job that you're sure will allow you to shine. But you want to hit the ground running by building good relationships with every important executive in the company—the very people you're going to be meeting with tomorrow in the MMCO executive conference room for your first major briefing and strategy session. What better way to establish an immediate rapport with your new bosses than to walk into the meeting knowing their names so well that an introduction is almost superfluous? Any new hire is an unknown quantity until people see him in action; nothing could be more reassuring to them than feeling like the new guy is so comfortable to be around that it seems like he's been working there for years.

You were talking to Mary in Human Resources the other day and mentioned that you'd like to have a copy of the MMCO annual report. She popped one in the mail. The package arrived today, and the annual report had just what you were hoping for: photos of the company's top players. There's Dave Wiseman (chief operating officer), John Murphy (founder and chief executive officer), your boss, Bill Simpson (chief financial officer), Barbara Lambert (chief information officer), Mary Curtis (director of Human Resources), and Mark Donahue (director of Sales and Marketing). By applying the NAME technique tonight to those photos, you'll be able to walk into the meeting and identify Dave, John, Bill, Barbara, Mary and Mark on sight, as well as greet them gracefully, by name, the moment you walk in the door. Get ready to NOMINATE, ARTICULATE, MORPH and ENTWINE!

**THE CONFERENCE ROOM CHALLENGE**

## DAVE

He might be the high-powered COO of the venerable Murphy's Manufacturing Corporation, but Dave's just a regular-looking guy. So, what can we NOMINATE about his face? As I explained in the NAME chapter, *any* feature can be nominated. In this case, let's go with Dave's unremarkable nose. Which turns out not to be all that pedestrian if you focus on it and start to ARTICULATE what you see: the tip has an angular, almost diamond-shaped quality.

You've NOMINATED Dave's nose, and ARTICULATED a description of it in order to secure it more firmly in your memory. Now let's discuss some possible MORPHS of his name. If you were meeting Dave at a party and were using the FACE technique, your mental COMMENT might have linked Dave to the story of David and Goliath. That would have given the name some resonance for you. We're using the NAME technique, though, and the story of David and Goliath has too many details. By focusing on just the image of a slingshot, though, you can conjure up the name David and you'll need something as tangible as a slingshot for the ENTWINING stage.

Another possible MORPH for Dave is "shave," which would lead you to an image of a razor. Whenever possible, I prefer MORPHS to begin with the same letter as the actual name. Therefore I like to MORPH Dave into "dive," symbolized by a diving board. This MORPH leaves less room for confusion.

On the one hand, we've NOMINATED and ARTICULATED Dave's nose; on the other is the MORPH of his name, dive/diving board. Now it's time to ENTWINE, completing the NAME process. Look at Dave's photo and imagine a diving board jutting straight out from where his nose should be. Not just any old board, but one that satisfies the A NOVEL COLOR PICTURE requirement. Let's pick up the "L" for Ludicrous in NOVEL: someone has just jumped off the board, the end of it diamond-shaped, leaving it wildly wagging up and down, throwing water off and making a silly "boing" sound as it smacks into Dave's forehead and whacks him on the teeth.

How can we add COLOR to this NOVEL PICTURE? The diving board is covered with a bright blue rubber surface with tiny raised bubbles to provide better traction.

By translating the staid photo of Dave into an image of him being battered by a bright blue diving board protruding from the center of his

face, you've made him unforgettable. When you go into that meeting tomorrow and encounter him face-to-face, there's no way you're going to fall into the deep end and start desperately splashing around trying to grasp his name. Stop now, close your eyes and take a moment to visualize our NAME sequence for Dave.

## JOHN

Let's do John's nose, too! In fact, let's do the noses of everybody in the room! Just kidding. But we could if we wanted to. That's the beauty of NAME: Each nose would have a different MORPH attached to it, making it utterly distinct from all the other noses in the room.

But forget John's nose. His whole head is so distinctive, it just begs to be NOMINATED. We *could* choose another feature, but none of them say John Murphy, chief executive officer of Murphy's Manufacturing Corporation, quite like his bald pate does. Any feature can be NOMINATED, but if nature provides something eye-catching, don't fight it.

What can be ARTICULATED about John's dome? It's a smooth, pink, almost perfect oval.

How shall we MORPH his name? An obvious choice would be long-johns, but I try to avoid using clothing as MORPHS, just as I try to avoid doing the laundry. To me, both are boring. If you're interested in fashion, though, clothing might be extremely useful. In my mind, a more vivid MORPH would be john, as in toilet. Yes, the word has an almost limitless potential for tasteless, disgusting imagery, but that's the beauty of it. We're going for *memorable* here, not dainty.

Once you've chosen john as your MORPH and are ready to ENTWINE, you can make the image as nice or nasty as your sensibility allows. My living is based in part on my ability to use the NAME technique under extreme pressure—one failure with it could spoil a whole performance. As a result, I tend to push my MORPHS to extremes when it comes to ENTWINING them. Meeting an individual named John at a cocktail party, you're probably fine making a simple connection to "toilet" as the MORPH for John. At one of my performances recently, though, there were *nine* men in the audience named John. Under this kind of pressure, I would ENTWINE John's NOMINATED feature, his head, with the MORPH for his name, a john, by imagining the swirling contents of a just-flushed toilet slopping around his pink, round dome.

I can hear readers groaning in disgust at this point. He's gone too far! Agreed. You don't have to get that detailed in your imagining. You can be much more decorous in your ENTWINING, relying on the image of John's pink head in place of an immaculate white porcelain toilet bowl. If it works, that's fine. But I've got a feeling that going the down and dirty ENTWINING route is the best way to ensure that when you walk into that MMCO conference room you'll be able to immediately extract John's name from memory. Even though you may not want to, stop, go back to his photo and visualize.

## BILL

The first thing I notice is the long, straight vertical line from the bottom of Bill's cheek to the top of his forehead on the left side of this photo. Any artist, from a caricaturist to Picasso, would latch on to that line immediately if the goal were to capture the essential Bill in a few quick pencil strokes. In NOMINATING this facial line, I've also ARTICU-LATED something about it, simply because the line required a bit more description than saying "chin" or "ears."

Bill's name could be MORPHED into "dollar bill." But even though I've used that image in the past, I'm not too thrilled with it: it's a small, flat, rectangular, inanimate piece of paper. It's the details of a MORPH, and the ensuing ENTWINING, that make the image memorable. Vagueness is your memory's enemy. There's also not much action implicit in a dollar bill. It can be folded or waved, but those are things done *to* the bill, not things it does or is used for naturally. Which is why I like to MORPH the name Bill directly into a bird's bill. Not just any bird's bill—though they're all much more action-oriented than a limp piece of paper bearing George Washington's likeness—a yellow, cartoony bill like Daffy Duck's.

ENTWINING a clacking, quacking duck's bill with the feature of Bill's face we've NOMINATED isn't hard. Just imagine that nice, straight line at the side of his face being snapped at and nibbled on as the bill works its way up to his forehead. Don't worry, your natural memory will make sure you don't walk into that meeting tomorrow, spy the gentleman with the ruler-straight chin-to-forehead line and say, "How are you, Jack?" because you were thinking, "Quack"! However, to be sure of that, take a moment and visualize.

**BARBARA**

What would a computer see if it were breaking down Barbara's face to make a digital eigenface model used in face-recognition technology? Several areas of intense light and dark contrasts, particularly her eyes. Let's NOMINATE them and ARTICULATE why they are so noticeable. Barbara's eyes appear to be widely spaced, which makes them stand out separately, and their darkness is heightened by the prominent twin patches of skin between her eyelids and eyebrows.

Years ago, I might have MORPHED her name into the word "bra," especially if I had NOMINATED her two eyes. It would have been easy to ENTWINE the two by imagining her penetrating eyes burning holes through the bra cups covering them. Come to think of it, that's a pretty good application of NAME. But nowadays I avoid the Barbara/bra MORPH just as I've quit using John/long-johns; clothing is inert and requires action to be performed *on* it (Barbara's eyes are doing the work in this one). Now I almost exclusively MORPH Barbara into barbed wire—barbed wire is so bristly and dangerous that imagining it in the context of someone's face implies more than enough violence being done to human skin. And that meets the requirements of A NOVEL COLOR PICTURE. I wince just thinking of how you could ENTWINE barbed wire with Barbara's eyes: let's just leave it at strands of gleaming silver wire ringed around her eye sockets, keeping intruders away, yet digging into her skin slightly, drawing a few beads of blood.

Just checking: Are you actually taking a minute to visualize the images for each person in the room? Or are you just gliding along, scanning the text and photos? Don't let it be the latter. If you're not building an image in your mind for each person, this conference room meeting is going to end badly. Go ahead and visualize!

## MARY

My eyes were immediately attracted to Mary's lower lip. In fact, I focused on it so closely that I was reminded of the danger of concentrating too intensely on a single feature to the exclusion of any other. Obsessing on one feature removes it from the context of the rest of the face. When you see Mary, you need to see the NOMINATED feature practically waving a flag among all the others. When you walk into that conference-room meeting, focusing exclusively on an individual feature without taking into account how it relates to the features around it can give you a roomful of disembodied noses, chins and eyebrows. Think back to the image of Dave and the diving board: the board was swinging up and down and

hitting his forehead and teeth. The interplay of features is important.

Let's look at Mary's face some more. Sometimes a good trick is to look for basic shapes. Do you see any simple, geometric shapes? I see her cheeks and chin as a set of three circles. It's a little abstract, but just for a challenge let's NOMINATE and ARTICULATE something about this trio of rounded forms, her small chin and larger cheeks. MORPH-ING the name Mary is pretty simple: I can't think of a more active, colorful equivalent than merry-go-round. You can ENTWINE Mary's NOMINATED feature and her name-MORPH by envisioning the poles and gaudily painted wooden horses of a merry-go-round going up and down and moving in circles around her rounded cheeks and chin. Add a little calliope music as the horses—painted yellow, blue, red and green—move up and down, squashing into her skin, and I think you've got a sufficiently ludicrous scenario to qualify as A NOVEL COLOR PICTURE. Take a moment now to visualize, and it will ensure that in the conference-room meeting you'll grab the gold ring . . . by remembering Mary's name.

## MARK

It looks like every day is a good hair day for Mark. Even his mustache looks great. So let's make use of it by NOMINATING his mustache. What can we ARTICULATE about it? Looks like he's got multiple colors going on in there: brown, white, silver and tan. The mustache is bushy enough to hide his upper lip—no Ted Turner via Douglas Fairbanks Jr. here.

A terrific MORPH for the name Mark is Magic Marker, because it combines both color and action. Indulge your inner child who delights in defacing photos by doing the obvious ENTWINING of Mark's NOMINATED mustache and a Magic Marker. Imagine a purplish-pink marker scribbling over Mark's mustache, maybe even adding some Groucho Marx glasses along the way. You might have to hide a smile when you see Mark in the conference room tomorrow, but you'll know where to find his name.

If you were truly preparing for a big meeting by going over photos in an annual report, you'd review the six photos now to see whose name didn't instantly come to mind. This way you could embellish the MORPHING and ENTWINING to make the memory stronger. But for now, let's see where you stand. Who are the people below?

Did you miss a name or two? That's okay. In fact, contrary to what you might think, it's great. Feeling a little frustrated can bring a motivational drive to your memory. An emotional reaction like that means you'll attach even more significance when you review the photos again, which will push the names even deeper into your memory. It's also a chance to freshen up your MORPHS and tweak the process of ENTWINING to create even more vivid impressions. My clients who experience too much early success are the ones who I worry about. The names come so easily that they're not securely tethered in memory and might slip away.

Oh, and by the way, who are these people?

If you had any trouble recalling names in either group of six, go back and review their identifications. Break down the way you used the NAME technique and try to figure out which step needs a little more work before you've got a solid grip on the name.

---

When forced to meet several people at once:
- Slow it down: Impose your own pace, do your own introductions, collect business cards.
- When possible, get a list of attendees to prepare MORPHS in advance.
- When possible, get photos in advance to MORPH and ENTWINE.

---

# NAME TECHNIQUE:
# THE TROUBLESHOOTING GUIDE

### TAKING-IT-FOR-GRANTED PROBLEMS

• Nonexistent technique. You take an easy name for granted: "He's got the same first name as mine!" Neglecting to MORPH and ENTWINE means trouble.

• Going by serendipitous seating. Sometimes two Bobs sit next to each other—which is fine ("The two Bobs!") until they mingle with others. Then you're lost. Sometimes John and Wayne sit next to each other, but before you can say, "Howdy, pardners," they've changed places.

• Mixing up FACE and NAME. Friends or celebrities are okay for cross-referencing a name for use with FACE, but not for gaining the long-term power of NAME.

### MORPHING PROBLEMS

• Weak MORPH. Yes, I've recommended that your MORPHS have a personal significance if possible, but even if you're a financial expert, a piece of paper that's supposed to signify a "bill" seems pretty lifeless to me. A wild, quacking bill is more memorable.

• Weak MORPH. You can MORPH Dave into "shave" and picture an electric razor humming next to his face, but that may just be too tame. Why not imagine it chewing up his cheeks? You can MORPH Dave into "dove," but did you picture a bird sitting on his head? Two problems there: the bird's not ENTWINED with his features, and there's nothing to make this bird specifically a *dove* in your mind. Better to have that dove coming out of a magician's hat or holding an olive branch in its beak.

• Giving up on a MORPH. If the name seems long, break it up into individual syllables. Or just get close to the name and your natural memory may surprise you. Microphone will serve you equally well for Michael, Mike, Mikey or Mikhail. Don't worry about being exact.

### ENTWINING PROBLEMS

• Weak linkage. Losing a name? Go back and add color and emotion.

• Nonlinkage, or adjacency instead of ENTWINING. For instance, a fern next to the woman rather than ENTWINED with a specific feature.

• Isolated linkage. Remembering the nose but not in relation to the face. If you focus solely on a woman's hair—to the exclusion of everything else—and then she puts it up, you're lost.

PART THREE

# The New Memory Expert— You

**CHAPTER 12**

# Challenging Names, Challenging Faces

If you find yourself plunged into a meeting emergency—when you're confronted by seemingly impossible-to-remember names or faces—don't panic. The NAME technique will ride to the rescue.

"I had a long association with Chase Manhattan Bank and because of that association I was in David Rockefeller's company many times. I recall in particular a formal dinner at Versailles. Five hundred top political and business people in Paris were there. Whether it was the French people who attended the party, the American business people on our board or young officers, David always remembered the right name. He was able to interact extraordinarily effectively."

—Jim Borden, Executive Vice President, Fleet Global Markets

I've already shown you how to remember a dozen of the most common names in America. That's what we accomplished by using NOMINATE, ARTICULATE, MORPH and ENTWINE—the NAME technique—to memorize the folks in the "Guess Who's Coming to Dinner" chapter and in our "Conference Room" visit. But don't get the impression that simple, commonplace names are all that NAME can handle. Now you're well armed to handle the names you're most likely to encounter professionally and socially. But the beauty of NAME is that it works regardless of how difficult the name might be, no matter how daunting the array of faces before you might seem. Below are a few guys who will *really* put the technique through its paces.

Imagine you're making the first of what will become an annual meeting with these gentlemen—and imagine your apprehension about remembering their names and keeping them straight if you were encountering them before having read this book!

They are, left to right, Masayuki Ito, Hideki Mitsuhashi and Kennichi Watanabe, executives in the New York headquarters of a Japanese-owned financial institution. Not only are their names challenging for Westerners, their social customs related to using names in business set-

tings also require a bit of extra attention. Many Japanese executives in the U.S. bring with them the tradition in their own country of using their last names almost exclusively for business dealings. If you hear only one name in a business introduction, it's certainly the last name. But with equal certainty, you'll also be given a business card (make sure, if you're meeting with representatives from a Japanese corporation, to have plenty of your own business cards to offer in exchange and as a sign of respect).

My own approach to meeting Japanese executives and the whole first-name/last-name question is: they're in America, and the usual practice here is to quickly move to using first names. Picking up on this, some Japanese businessmen will use an Americanized first name—but maintain some uniformity with Japanese tradition by forming it from their last names, i.e., Mr. Mitsuhashi might say, "Call me Mitch." But eventually, especially if you're careful to make it clear that you prefer to be on a first-name basis as a matter of doing business with everyone, *and you and the executive are of equal standing,* it can be a simple matter and no breach of etiquette to refer to Japanese executives by their given first names. If I'm in a meeting that includes several Americans and one Japanese businessman, I try to speak with all of the Americans first, making a point of using their first names, so that the Japanese visitor will see that we're all using first names and follow suit. Even "Mitch" Mitsuhashi has come around to being called Hideki, seeing the sports pages in New York making frequent reference to baseball pitcher Hideki Irabu.

So how can we memorize the names of Hideki and his associates? Won't it be almost impossible? Nobody's got a name even close to Tom-as-in-Tommy-gun, or Sue-as-in-Sioux.

It will indeed take more time, but the technique stays the same.

The NAME technique will allow you to memorize their names and faces just as easily as when you handled your fellow diners in the "Guess Who's Coming to Dinner" chapter. Let's get going!

## HIDEKI MITSUHASHI

This man is a snappy dresser, but as you know by now, NOMINATING clothing is taboo. Fixing on his tie with the bands of fine horizontal stripes as a NOMINATED feature might get you through the meeting with his name intact in your memory. But it wouldn't help if you ran into him at the golf course a week from now, or when you return next year for your annual meeting at the company. If he's still wearing the same clothes a year from now that he's wearing here, don't bother trying to get his name, get him a tailor.

A physical characteristic is what we're looking for, as usual. I recommend choosing to focus on this man's eyebrows because it's easy to ARTICULATE a few observations about them: they're thick and rectangularly shaped. They also seem to be high on his brow—the frames of his eyeglasses don't obscure them at all.

An obvious MORPH of his first name, Hideki, into a visual equivalent would be simply to capitalize on his shared name with pitcher

**REMEMBER EVERY NAME EVERY TIME**

Hideki Irabu. You could use baseballs to connote his profession, and ENTWINE the eyebrows and baseballs by imagining two baseballs lodged in his brow, almost totally obscuring the eyebrows, as if they had been fired by a hard-throwing pitcher and simply stuck in his skull. You could ENTWINE the eyebrow hairs with the distinctive red stitches of a baseball. For me, though, the baseball MORPH isn't ideal. First of all, there are many, many pitchers in the big leagues, and while there's not much danger of seeing this man with the baseballs in his eyebrows and thinking "Pedro!" for Pedro Martinez, there's a good possibility you might think "Hideo!" for Hideo Nomo, another Japanese pitcher in the major leagues and whose first name is close to Hideki's.

*The MORPH doesn't need to be so detailed that it provides you with a precise spelling and pronunciation of the name; it only needs to approximate the name, getting close enough to allow your natural memory to kick in with the correct information.* Are you familiar with the Hide-a-key device for keeping a spare car key or house key in a location where you can find it in an emergency? It's a little box with a magnet that lets you affix it to the underside of a car, say, or to the back of an air-conditioning unit. Using Hide-a-key as the MORPH, you can EN-TWINE it with the NOMINATED characteristic by envisioning a Hide-a-key box nestled in each of his bushy eyebrows. To liven up the scenario, imagine him trying to extricate the Hide-a-keys from his eye-brows, wincing in pain as he pulls out hairs as well.

You may feel you're wobbly with pronunciations and don't trust your natural memory to adjust "Hide-a-key" to the name's correct pronunciation, Hee-DECK-ee. But try it. You may find that your memory will surprise you. Nevertheless, we can use NAME to get even closer to the name. The MORPH comes almost in tandem with the ENTWINING: We want to imagine him enacting the phrase "He deck eel" (or "He decks an eel"), so conjure up an image of him punching out eels where his eyebrows were. An alternative: his eyebrows come to life and deck an E—a giant letter E that seems to have wandered in off the set of *Sesame Street.* If you would never use the word "deck" to mean "punch," then slam the point home by imagining our friend gripping a deck of cards in his hands and using them to flatten the big E.

Make a specific choice right now, and ENTWINE.

## MASAYUKI ITO

This looks like a terribly difficult first name, right? You're probably gazing longingly at the last name and thinking of Judge Ito from the O. J. Simpson murder trial and how much easier it would be to remember a three-letter name.

Let's make Masayuki easy, too. First, of course, comes NOMINATING a feature. Yes, he's the only man in the trio who's not wearing a tie, thus exposing his neck, but there's no guarantee that the next time you see Masayuki he won't be wearing a tie or a turtleneck. His bangs are a better choice— he's the youngest of the three men, and his bangs emphasize his youth. But they're not the best choice, because a year from now—or a week from now—he might have a different haircut. The mole near his left nostril is much more likely to have permanent residence. We've already ARTICULATED its location, but let's say a little more: the mole isn't as dark as those that some people have, and it lines up almost directly below his pupil when he's looking straight ahead.

Now comes the challenging bit: MORPHING Masayuki. How about "marsala ukie"—as in the wine and mushrooms dish and a teeny, tiny ukulele. The ENTWINING could call for him to use the ukie to dig at the mole, causing an eruption of marsala to spill out of it.

But here's the MORPH that I've actually used for this name. Finding MORPHS that have a repulsive quality makes them more memorable, so a MORPH that refers to a repugnant time in American history is going to be—because of its very awfulness—more easily remembered.

The owner of a Southern plantation was known among the slaves as Massa. Putting that to use here, I imagine the Massa in a white linen suit and hat, with a gigantic key that's so heavy it drags across the ground behind him on a heavy key chain. But it's not just any key—this Massa's key is formed into a U shape, like a horseshoe. It is the Massa's U key. It can be ENTWINED by envisioning the Massa using the key to dig out the mole on Mr. Ito's face, doing damage to the skin and even drawing blood that drips onto the Massa's white suit, but never quite excavating the mole. Massa U key. Masayuki. There, that wasn't so hard, was it?

Choose one of these scenarios and make A NOVEL COLOR PICTURE.

### KENNICHI WATANABE

Let's not NOMINATE a particular feature here—let's go with the whole head! We could say that this man's head is almost rectangular, with the long dimples under his prominent cheekbones only heightening the linear effect. (There's your ARTICULATION.) Here's option number one: see his head in the shape of a soup can. I'd use something distinctive, like the red and white Campbell's Soup can. It's a can with a problem that makes it unbelievably itchy, so itchy that he can't resist scratching it, especially right under the cheekbones, where he's dug out two hollow areas. You might start to feel your skin crawling a little yourself whenever you see Kennichi, but it's not likely you'll forget the soup CAN with the ITCHY problem, or fail to convert CAN-ITCHY to Kennichi.

A completely different option: "Kennichi" (Ken-EE-chee) is awfully close to the name of the musician Kenny G. Visualize one of Kenny G's saxophones: Kennichi's blowing his sax through a hole in his cheek. Given that image, the next time you see Mr. Watanabe and for a nanosecond worry about recalling his first name, that image of the saxophone will make your memory shout out the name. It will be music to your ears—and to his when you confidently say, "Hello, Kennichi," as you shake hands. Pick your option and visualize.

Now that you've got all three Japanese businessmen's names fixed in your mind, it's time to meet them as a group once more. Okay, who are they?

# Okay, So You Skipped
# Foreign-Language Studies

Because of past bad experiences with trying to pronounce foreign names or words, some readers are going to remain skeptical of using the NAME technique with names from other countries. Especially if, instead of having the MORPHING simplicity of Tom = Tommy gun, they have to come up with a multistep narrative, a complicated visualization of "He decks the letter E."

Well, in the increasingly globalized economy, you're probably going to have opportunities more and more often to interact with folks from overseas. Enhancing your career by remembering and using first names with them should be just as effective as with American executives—if not even *more* appreciated. Don't give up on foreign names. If you know that people from another country are going to be at your next meeting or business affair, obtain a guest list the day before and study it to create potential MORPHS so that you can go into action ready to succeed. The list may not give you pronunciations, but you're still way ahead of the game. It *does* take time to create MORPHS with foreign names, but the ENTWINING can go quickly once you've got them. So make *a special effort to obtain the guest list in advance* if you know you're going to face a challenge from overseas.

Depending on the ethnic group you're dealing with, you could find some common sounds that many names in the culture share (such as the "ee" at the end of the names of the Japanese businessmen we just met). Having MORPHS for those sounds ready in advance will pay off. Here's a little crib sheet of possible MORPHS for common vowel endings that you might encounter:

    ah—tongue depressor
    ay—hay
    ee—eel
    oh—oats
    oo—goo

At your next opportunity, successfully rattle off several names of European or Asian business executives whom you've just met and you'll have them—and your co-workers—saying, "oo . . . ah!"

## CIRCUS MAXIMUS

We've just dealt with challenging names. What if the names are easy, but it's the faces that are hard? I love this poster because at first glance it looks like an array of faces no one could ever keep straight—isn't everyone in it just balding and wearing a mustache? It looks like a police lineup after the Lincoln assassination. But upon closer examination, each man in the illustration turns out to be readily identified and committed to memory using the NAME technique. I'll take you rapid-fire through these faces and names, giving you one-line NOMINATIONS and ARTICULATIONS, and one-line MORPHS that will get you started on the ENTWINING. Soon you'll have them jumping through hoops like a lion-tamer putting his cats through their paces in the center ring.

Let's start with the easy ones: the non-Ringlings.

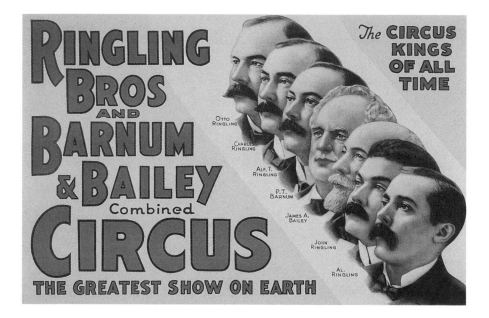

- **P.T. Barnum** (fourth from left) has a high forehead, fringed with silver hair. See John Kennedy's famous World War II vessel, "PT"-109, riding the crest of his hair.
- **James Bailey** (fifth from left) has a grayish beard and dark eyebrows. The name James MORPHS to "chains," which can be seen clanking in his silvery beard.

Now for the Brothers Ringling, who initially look like quintuplets. When faces are virtually identical, NOMINATE the physical distinctions between individuals, no matter how minor. It will be a temptation, but don't memorize these people by their locations in the lineup, because in real life, as you might have noticed, people tend to move around.

- **Otto** (first from left) has the pointiest mustache of the group. That's good, because his first name can MORPH to "otter," which has a dark tail that will look nice wagging under his nose.
- **Charles** (second from left) has a protruding lower lip that noticeably peeks out from under his mustache. His first name MORPHS to "chars," which unfortunately means our friend's lip is going to glow redder and redder until it finally burns out and turns a charred black, with a wisp of smoke rising from it.
- **Alf** (third from left) has long eyelashes, which are going to have to work overtime to keep the fettuccini "Alfredo" in them from dripping into his eyes.
- **John** (second from right) has a nice, full head of black hair—pity about it being located in the toilet bowl ("john") ringing his head as his hair is flushed away.
- **Al** (first from right) has an especially droopy mustache, which you could envision as the wings of a bird. The wings of an "owl," to be precise.

Once again, don't just read. Picture each for a split second.

That's it. The entire septet of the original bosses at the Ringling Bros. and Barnum & Bailey Circus. Now, without looking back at the poster, try to answer these questions:

- What's the name of the person with the fullest head of hair?
- Who's got the droopiest mustache?
- Whose eyelashes are dripping with white sauce?
- When you see a pointy mustache, what does that remind you of?

**CHALLENGING NAMES, CHALLENGING FACES**

Maybe you got some or all of those correct. I hope so. Here's another test: Look at the poster again.

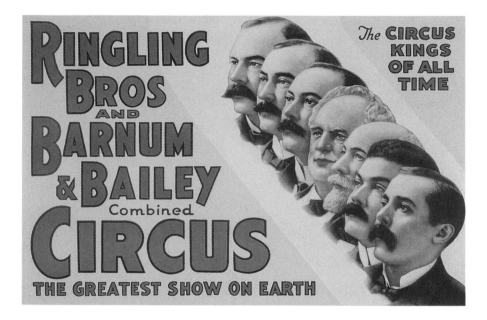

Remember the NAME technique as it was applied—even a condensed form—to each individual. For instance, check out that pointy mustache on the far left—wasn't it supposed to look like an animal's tail? Which animal? Hmmmm. . . . wasn't it an otter? Oh, yeah, that's Otto! How many can you recall?

If you had some success with this Circus Maximus memory quiz, congratulate yourself! I only provided the barest outline for applying the NAME technique here. You and your imagination did the rest.

Now you're ready to create your own challenges. Does your company have a face book, a photo guide to employees? There might be 200 in the book, which sounds daunting. But, hey, you just memorized the names of three Japanese businessmen and five look-alike Ringling brothers—imagine how much easier it will be when you add women to the mix, along with ethnic diversity and a wide range of ages.

Either get your own copy of your company's face book, or if they don't have one, make a copy of several pages from the book where a colleague works. Conventions or conferences that you might attend often publish guides that have photos of the participants—those are another good source. Write a MORPH for each name next to the person's photo. Then start using the NAME technique, 10 people at a time. Memorize the first 10, then the next day review what you learned. If you've lost a couple of names, try to figure out why. Was the ENTWINING too tame, with A NOVEL COLOR PICTURE that wasn't strong enough? Rework it, amping up the degree that it's Active, New, Obscene, Violent, Emotional or Ludicrous.

Once you've got the first 10 names and faces down, do another 10, then review all 20. Once you've confirmed that you know all 20, add another 10 and establish that you've got all 30.

Now the procedure changes. Move on to the next 10, leaving behind the very first group of 10 so that you're never juggling more than 30 names at a time. Three reviews of each dollop of 30 names ought to suffice before you advance another step. Once a month, go through all the names and faces you've memorized so far, then start over with the 10-20-30 process until you've got all the names. For a group of 200, I'd expect that by the end of a few months of practicing twice a week you'd have all the names. (If I were there at your side to help out, it would go much more quickly. A client of mine, a company chairman, once needed to memorize 150 names—75 employees and their spouses. I admit that he was really sharp, but he had them cold in just three 90-minute sessions.)

If you used your own company's face book for the project, celebrate by inviting a friend over for a tour of the company—and introduce everyone you meet by name to your friend.

*In fact, the introducing of friends and clients to people in your office isn't just a way of celebrating your new knowledge.* If you're in a management position, it's a wonderful way to show the people who work for you how personally connected to them you feel. A CEO client of mine makes a point of periodically taking visitors around the office and introducing them to the staff—several dozen people on his floor alone—both as a way of refreshing his memory of his employees' names and as a subtle but effective morale-booster.

To keep the names and faces on your photo list fresh in your mind, review it once a month for a few months. Use people's names in the office as often as possible. After a while, there's a good chance that you'll notice you don't even have to consult the NAME technique when you see someone from the face book—you simply know the name, instantly. Congratulations. You've just shifted into true long-term memory!

---

- You can MORPH *any* name.
- You can ARTICULATE about *any* face.
- Some names—and faces—require extra time and practice.
- If you struggle with doing the NAME technique on the fly, prep work will be a great help.

---

With our increasingly global economy, gaining proficiency at remembering names that are foreign to you is likely to become an essential skill. And it will make remembering names commonly found in America seem like child's play.

# CHAPTER 13

# I Need It All!

Sometimes the first name is just the
first thing you want to be able to
remember—followed by last name,
spouse's name, kids' names and maybe
even the last topic you two discussed.
Here's how to remember it *all*.

"When a customer comes in, if I can walk up and say, 'Bill, how
are you? How are the kids? Joan's doing okay?' that's great.
When I call one of my employees' homes at night and the wife
answers the phone, if I can remember her name I think that goes
a long way. Can I show you that we have less turnover with people whose names I can remember? I can't show you those numbers. But I'm sure it's true."

—*Michael Bloomberg, Founder and Chairman, Bloomberg LP*

You're going to play golf today with a group that will include a fellow
named Rich Connor, who last played with you and several business
contacts about a year ago in this same country-club tournament.
Rich runs a rival outfit, which led to some good-natured kidding on
the first few holes during that round. On the back nine, he hinted
that he'd like to talk to you about taking over one of his troubled di-
visions, but you didn't handle the overture too gracefully. You were
so surprised—and not sure you were the right person to whip the di-

vision into shape—that you didn't even give Rich a chance to show his cards a little more clearly. Instead, you acted like he was just kidding again and laughed it off.

What a difference a year makes. You've learned more about Rich's company, and about the still-troubled division. Now you're convinced that it would be a great fit, and an opportunity unlike any you'd be likely to tackle in your present situation. In other words, you want to make a big impression on Rich, whom you've only met that one time a year ago, in the hope that he'll be reminded of his previous interest in you and perhaps introduce the job possibility again. You want to be able to speak with him in a casual, friendly way that shows you're really on the ball. You'd like to have his whole name on the tip of your tongue (in case you have to introduce him to someone) as if you've known him for years, as well as his wife's name, his kids' names and even something you discussed during that round a year ago, something that it might surprise him to find you still remembered.

A quick call to a friend at Rich's company turns up the names of Rich's wife, Claire, and children, Bridget and Cara, all of which you had forgotten before you got off the eighteenth green last year. But what was it you and he talked about last year? A quick glance at your Palm Pilot notes from that day remind you: the long-planned family vacation in London that he had just returned from.

Normally, you might be able to just pound the information into your head by rote (a.k.a. Repeat Obsessively Till Exam). But there are half a dozen other golfers in your two foursomes who could be important business connections, and you want to have some info about them in mind as well. You can't memorize it all by rote in the short time you've got until teeing off.

You saw a photo of Rich in the business section of the local paper a few days ago and saved it. Now a session with the NAME technique will allow you to get his first name down pat so that if you don't run into him until you're among the golfers waiting at the first tee, you'll be able to pick him out easily and greet him by name.

# The NAME Technique Bonus

Here's the good news: you can also use the NAME technique to memorize all the other information that you want to have readily available during your conversation with him.

The newspaper photo of Rich shows him wearing glasses with rather large lenses. Since it's such a recent photo, you can be reasonably certain he hasn't changed his appearance drastically. My favorite way to MORPH the name "Rich" is to use an image of gold. But not just any old gold nuggets; I use a rare coin in my act known as a "missing motto" twenty-dollar gold piece. It was designed by St. Gaudens and is a beautiful piece of change. Instead of having the usual milled rim, the rim is smooth except for the letters spelling out E PLURIBUS UNUM, with a star separating each letter, for a total of thirteen stars.

Two of these lovely gold coins, sadly, have been ruined just to make Rich's eyeglasses: the coins have been cut into the shape of his lenses and pressed into his eye sockets, blocking his sight. That's the NAME technique for first names. Let's make another strange adjustment to his eyewear. Each coin has a tiny conning tower atop it, rising up to his hairline, with a submarine periscope wheeling around and around. Your imaginary scenario, inspired from just looking at the newspaper photo of Rich, unfolds some more: the bottoms of the gold coins with the E*P*L*U*R*I*B*U*S*U*N*U*M* lettering are biting into the skin of his cheeks until a strange woman comes to his rescue and takes off

**I NEED IT ALL!**

the glasses with a hand that's perfectly clear—in fact, her entire body is clear. The strange thing (as if the imagery isn't strange enough already—now here's where we get *really* hallucinatory) is that the clear woman is in the middle of giving birth to a scale model of a bridge. Not just any bridge, but one that has long curls of hair. Not just any bridge with curls, but one that's holding hands with a car that *also* has curls and—believe it or not—is towing a rapidly disintegrating model of Big Ben.

So that's the story. Glasses with gold coins and conning towers. Clear woman, giving birth to a bridge covered with curly hair. Holding hands with equally curly-haired car that's towing a Big Ben. Do you see it? Great! You've also got all you need to know before heading over to the country club.

Gold = Rich
Conning tower = Connor
Clear woman = Wife Claire
Bridge with curls = Daughter Bridget
Car = Second daughter Cara
Big Ben = Trip to London

Here's an amazing thing about the way memory and the NAME technique work. Because you've focused so much time and mental energy on Rich Connor and details about his life, it doesn't even faze you when you arrive at the golf course, see a guy who looks an awful lot like Rich and realize that it *is* him—but he's not wearing his glasses! Those crucial glasses!

Everything you memorized depended on them! But wait: you've already recognized Rich. The process of looking at his photo and studying both it and the information you wanted to retain has subtly imprinted his face in your memory. Your imagination kicks in, planting those crazy coin-laden, conning-tower-topped glasses on his face, and the whole memory-prompting scenario falls into place.

You've still got all the information you need, ready to be called into action as you greet Rich by name. Before you know it—right there by the golf cart—you're asking him about Claire and Bridget and Cara and wondering if they're planning to go back to London anytime soon. Whew! That's taken care of. Now that you don't have to be concerned about remembering details about Rich Connor, it's time to worry about your slice.

# Last Recall

In the previous chapter, you memorized the first name of a Japanese businessman named Masayuki. It's pretty clear from that experience that you can remember any challenging name if you work at it. Up until now, we've been concentrating on first names, because I hear again and again from clients that remembering first names is what they want and need in order to successfully interact in today's business world. But there will be situations where you'll want to remember last names. They take more time than first names, but with the NAME technique they're no problem.

Last names tend to be longer than the shortened first names people often use. The extra syllables do demand more effort in applying the NAME technique. Last names are also much more varied than first names. If you memorize the MORPHS listed in the back of this book, that's about fifty percent of the people you're ever going to meet. Last names have so much variety that memorizing an equal number of MORPHS wouldn't take you past "Bates" in most phone books.

Last names are like first names in that they either have meaning, we can find meaning in them, or we can impose meaning on them.

The first two groups enable you to think about them in advance of a meeting. The last names that already have meaning are ones like Hill, Armstrong, Taylor and Carpenter. They instantly paint a picture of a green mound, a bulging bicep, etc. The last names we can find meaning in already have strong associations for most people, whether the names remind them of presidents (Johnson, Kennedy, Bush) or corporate marketing (Colonel Sanders, Ford Motor Company, Mrs. Fields Cookies). Then there are the last names, the vast majority of them, that don't fit those two categories and need to be MORPHED into an easily visualized image. My name, Levy, is pronounced Lee-vee. If you knew I was a regular customer and you wanted to address me as "Mr. Levy," three MORPHS could spring to mind. After NOMINATING my hairline, say, you could then picture it as a *levee* with hordes of people standing on it waiting for the paddleboat the *Robt. E. Lee.* You could choose *Levi's* jeans and see them growing out of my head around the fringe of my hairline, with the copper rivets digging into my head. The third choice, and probably best because it comes closest to the actual pronunciation of my name, would be to see me as very *leafy,* with autumn leaves woven into my hairline like a laurel wreath.

In the give-and-take of social and business interaction, it's having a good memory for first names that impresses people and makes them feel flattered in a good way. Still, there are occasions when—as in the Rich Connor golf-date scenario the chapter started out with—you want to remember last names and more.

# The Domino: Effective

You know from this book's Prologue that you have the ability to remember a list of concrete images to form a story that is a guide to what you want to remember. When I was a kid, I memorized thirty objects as a stunt for my magic shows. You can do that, too, because now you have the techniques to accomplish it. You doubt it? Okay, let's prove it. As in the Prologue and the more recent golf-date example, this is just a matter of building a story, piece by interlocking piece. Or you could imagine it as a long line of dominoes, with each one that tips over making the next one tip, too, until the whole line has toppled.

No spoon-feeding on this one. No suggestions, no hints.

# You've Come So Far . . . Now Give *This* a Try!

Here's a list of thirty items. You'll note that each item is easy to see. Not every item is an object—like microphone. But every item *can* be seen—like rattlesnake. You can make up a real saga, with one item tied to the next, in less time than you think. Just link the items using the ideas you now know. You can recall everything on this list. Go on, try it!

| | | |
|---|---|---|
| Hourglass | VCR | Unicycle |
| Television | Rattlesnake | Sand |
| Sailboat | Coral | Lighthouse |
| Necklace | Champagne cork | Jellyfish |
| Pail | Cat | Brain |
| Parachute | Windshield | Lion |
| Butterfly wings | Football | Incandescent bulb |
| Owl | Octopus | Dam |
| Gyroscope | Microphone | Tape deck |
| Kangaroo | Keys | Airplane |

If you can do this (and I know you can), then you'll be able to do *any* set of items, or any set of names. You may have seen that a few items were MORPHs of names: Pail for Paul, Owl for Al, Coral (Carol), Brain (Brian), Necklace (Nicholas) and of course, Microphone (Mike).

Make sure you keep the distinctions clear, as in the case of a big lighthouse and a very small incandescent bulb. You must form a "bulb" image that won't mix you up down the road. And make sure your tape deck is for small music tapes, not those big videocassettes next to your VCR.

MORPH the names or ideas so that you can use them, all in a row, to make one long story. Make it active. Add color. You know what to do. By now you can make a small champagne cork as active as an octopus if you wish. If each item's clear and each link crisp, everything in your story will fall into place.

The list of thirty objects might have seemed arbitrary—well, let's be honest, it was arbitrary. It was an exercise, after all. But was it really so different, other than being longer, from the earlier list in the golf story? You memorized, in order, this list: coins, conning tower, clear woman, bridge, car, Big Ben. Far from being arbitrary, though, the shorter list was a key to everything you ever wanted to know about Rich Connor but were afraid you'd forget.

The list of thirty objects could just as easily have been a list of thirty MORPHS for things you wanted to remember about someone. Is someone out there yelling, " 'Easily?' There's nothing 'easily' about it! I've gotta MORPH all this stuff, then domino them into a story? It's too much work!"

The answer to that is, well, what are your options? If you have a list of items you want to remember in association with a particular person, just trying to rivet them into your brain by rote labor isn't a very secure way of accomplishing your goal. Using the NAME technique and the story form is work, yes, but it's more effective than all the alternatives.

But here's one labor-saving device for you. When you meet so many corporate executives, knowing someone's exact title is one more way to impress them, particularly when introducing one exec to another. Here's a ready reference for remembering many of the various titles you might encounter. Titles are a bit like first names: you can memorize in advance the MORPHS for the most frequently occurring ones and feel pretty confident that you're going to be able to handle confidently almost anything thrown your way without having to create MORPHS from scratch, under pressure. Here's your crib sheet:

> **Chairman:** Use a very specific chair that you're familiar with, and connect it to the MORPH of his name, which is already ENTWINED with a facial characteristic.
>
> **President:** A gift-wrapped present.
>
> **CEO:** The various chiefs in a company are distinguishable in their titles by the letter between the "C" and the "O," so I only concern myself with the middle words in their titles. I think of a very familiar briefcase to connote the "Executive" in Chief Executive Officer.
>
> **COO:** The O is for Operating, so I imagine a scalpel.

**CFO:** The image I use to connote "Financial" is an adding machine spitting a long stream of paper.

**CIO:** A computer monitor equals Information in my book.

**Director:** A riding crop and jodhpurs, in an homage to the flamboyant movie directors of yore.

**Vice President:** I alternate between using the image of a man in a tuxedo, i.e., a VIP, and picturing a vise like you'd find in a woodworking shop.

**VP—Sales:** The man in the tux (the VIP) is steering a sailboat (sales), with water splashing onto his nice tuxedo.

**VP—Marketing:** Here the VIP is pushing a shopping cart at the supermarket.

**VP—Human Resources:** Our very busy VIP is swinging a baseball bat and hitting a home run—known in the box-score as an HR.

**Executive VP:** The tuxedoed VIP with an X ray where his chest should be; or a vise holding a sheet of X-ray film.

**Senior VP:** MORPH "senior" into "señor," so let's bring back the man in the tux, wearing a decidedly nonformal sombrero. If you ENTWINE a sombrero-wearing, tuxedo-clad VIP with the MORPH for your target's name, you'll always know he's a senior vice president.

**Senior Executive VP:** Yikes, the sombrero-wearing Mr. VIP needs to eat a few quesadillas; his body is an X ray.

**Senior Executive VP—Sales:** He's a long way from a good meal now—Mr. VIP is out on a sailboat, getting splashed all over again. But at least the sombrero is keeping the sun off his face.

**Managing Director:** The initials are MD, so hang a stethoscope here.

**Partner:** Give this guy a cowboy hat and say, "Howdy, pardner."

Two other words that crop up in titles are "Global" and "U.S." To spark "Global," just picture a globe. For "U.S.," you can capture those initials by going with a red *union suit* with the back flap down. Imagining an American flag is tempting, but only choose that option if you're sure you're not dealing with a company that has overseas operations; otherwise, your mind will soon be studded with more symbols and designs than the flags at the United Nations and you won't be able to sort out who belongs where. Flags are tricky.

If you don't agree with any of the above suggestions, feel free to substitute your own. By now, you know what the strategy is: impose meaning on the vague or meaningless. Make it vivid; make it memorable.

At this point, you're perfectly capable of devising your own MORPHS for names, titles or companies. In fact, I'm feeling so good about what you've learned that I think you're ready for a major review of the folks we've met so far. Here are photos of all the people we've encountered in Part Two: the guests from "Guess Who's Coming to Dinner," the conference-room gang, the trio of Japanese businessmen and your golfing buddy.

Examine each face carefully, using NAME to find the names.

REMEMBER EVERY NAME EVERY TIME

I NEED IT ALL!

REMEMBER EVERY NAME EVERY TIME

I NEED IT ALL!

Did you forget anyone's name? If so, was there any pattern to the misses? Did you lose the names of the youngest people, or of the women? Did you forget names if they were for people who didn't seem clearly of importance in a business sense, like the people in the dinner party photo? Did you struggle with the earlier photos because you weren't as adept with NAME as you became later in Part Two?

Only *you* can tell where your weaknesses are (if you had any—many people will get all the photos right). I wish I could be there at your side to help fine-tune your education in NAME so that there was never a single glitch. But that last bit of polishing requires you to be your own teacher.

> • Any amount of information can be connected—one domino can topple another one, two, three or a hundred.

## REMEMBER *MY* NAME EVERY TIME

In addition to wanting to remember names, I think it's safe to say, we all want to *be remembered*. Surprise someone you've just met by remembering his name and you'll make a terrific impression. That simple act helps to make *you* memorable in his mind. But you can help your cause along—and do a favor to anyone who hasn't read this book and struggles to remember names—by offering them a mnemonic device to remember your name. My name, Levy, can be difficult to remember, or at least pronouncing it is a challenge (LEH-vee or LEE-vee), so, when meeting someone I could offer up one of two tips, to get my name pronounced correctly. I mention that when I ran for elementary school president in sixth grade, my slogan was "Leave a vote for Levy," or I say that a memory expert once told me that he remembers my name by thinking of me as "leafy."

When you use the FACE technique, you ASK about the other person's name as part of the memorization process. But the fact that the conversation has turned to the subject of names almost certainly means that the person you've just met will ask about your name as well. That's a subsidiary benefit of FACE: it allows you to impress your name on someone you've just met. You're doing them a favor by helping them to remember your name, and doing yourself a favor in the process. So find—or invent—some interesting stories about your own name.

Benjamin isn't an unusual name, but if we get into a conversation about it, I've got plenty that I can say. My name is Benjamin Levy—it's not only Jewish, it's about as Jewish as possible, containing two of the twelve tribes of Israel in one name. I was named after my grandfather, who liked to be called Ben. But I always disliked being called that because it led to places I didn't care for, whether it was the TV show *Gentle Ben,* or the horror-movie rat named Ben. If you get me into a conversation about my name, in other words, I can bring up biblical, genealogical, or pop cultural connections.

Similarly, when *you're* using the FACE technique and reach the COMMENT stage, you can help others to remember your name by giving them little conversational prods to make their own COMMENT. I met someone once whose name was Nick, and he mentioned that when he was young, kids called him Nickel Pickle. I haven't seen Nick in years, but I've never forgotten his name, thanks to the information he volunteered. I sometimes say that I rarely run into anyone named Benjamin and ask if they've met any Benjamins before. *That gets them to start cross-referencing my name in their minds, strengthening the memory of it.*

It's important to get your name across several times in the course of a conversation with someone you've just met if they're going to have any hope of remembering it. To get the ball rolling, I take a page from 007's book and put a spin on it, introducing myself as "Benjamin, Benjamin Levy." Another way to sprinkle your name into conversation is to quote someone else using it: "So my wife said to me, 'Benjamin . . .' " Then, of course, there's giving the other person your business card. When I was starting out, I thought that perhaps I had spent much too much money hiring a designer to come up with a very unusual, elegant, embossed business card for me ($2,000 is a lot for a business card). But in the end it was a great investment. Nearly everyone who got the card closely examined it, clearly saw my name and associated me with something new, different and of great quality. But don't assume that having even the most eye-catching business card is sufficient to cement your name in someone's memory. A follow-up phone call or e-mail within twenty-four hours, to say "thank you" or "it was a pleasure meeting you," puts the finishing touch on the memory. With luck, the people you meet will have as good a fix on *your name* as you, having read this book, will certainly have on theirs.

# CHAPTER 14

# If You Do Forget . . .

Ideally, you'll always be on your game,
with the FACE and NAME techniques
operating like well-oiled machinery.
But someone, somewhere, is going to
catch you off guard. Here's how to cope
when your mind goes blank.

"I used to be really good. I could remember your face, I could
remember your name. Now I meet so many different people.
You don't plan your own agenda. You're being taken in, you shake
hands, and you have so much on your mind, whether it's what
you're going to say or when your next flight is, that you can't pay
attention to the same degree as before."

—*Jolene Sykes, President of* Fortune *magazine*

A guy walks into a bar and sees a familiar face.

> First guy: "Frank, it's so good to see you again! You look great!
> You've changed your hair. You've changed your wardrobe.
> You've changed your glasses. How've you been, Frank?"
> Second guy: "I'm not Frank."
> First guy: "My God, you've even changed your name."

Well, that's one way of handling a Missing Name emergency. Obviously, this guy never studied the FACE or NAME technique. You're unlikely ever to use these methods and come up with an absolutely, not-even-close misidentification. If, using the NAME technique, you've MORPHED the name Bob into a bobsled and ENTWINED it by envisioning tiny bobsleds flying around the contours of his nose, there's no way you're going to run into Bob in the shopping mall and suddenly envision his ears as optic-yellow tennis balls and say, "Dennis, how are you?"

However, there is a chance that you might run into Bobsled Bob in the food court and, in that out-of-context setting, draw a complete blank. In order to prevent the odd embarrassing incident, it helps to make a habit of imagining people you know in a variety of settings and in different clothing. Compaq's Ben Rosen tells me this story on himself: "I've played in golf foursomes where I've been put together with three people over eighteen holes. Then we go into the locker room, change clothes and go into the lunchroom. I say to someone, 'Hi, I'm Ben Rosen.' And they say, 'I know. We've been playing golf together for the past four hours.' It's very embarrassing. I'm tempted to pull a Nelson Rockefeller and fall back on, 'Hiya,' without bothering to learn their names."

We all have busy lives, with a million things tugging on our minds and distracting us from the tasks at hand, so there's no telling when the Big Blank is going to hit. It could strike at work when you run into someone you've known for years in the lobby of your building, or at a party with someone you met recently but have just spent the past twenty minutes talking to. You never know when your mental gremlins are going to sabotage all your careful preparation for remembering names and faces.

I'm positive that drawing a name-blank is much, much less likely to happen to anyone fortified by the FACE and NAME techniques than to people who rely on their untrained memory. I wouldn't be surprised, in fact, to learn that it *never happens to you again*. But it helps to prepare for every eventuality, so I'd be remiss not to offer the best possible advice on dealing with a sudden memory shortfall. Much of it is based on conversations with CEOs in major U.S. corporations, who were good enough to share their strategies with me (yes, even the big boys have a lurking fear of not remembering a name and have developed coping tactics).

Before presenting you with the list of recommendations, though, let me offer one irrevocable rule about what *not* to do: *never guess.* The only thing worse than letting an acquaintance know that you can't remember his name is to let him know that he's so far from meriting your notice that you've randomly assigned him someone else's name. It makes the other person feel about an inch tall—which will match their opinion of you for years to come.

Now on to some solutions that you might want to consider:

# Beat 'Em to the Punch

Charles Bronfman, co-chairman of the Seagram Company Ltd., says that remembering and using names in conversations is a "very, very important" business tool. He tells me that his memory for names and faces has been enormously improved by our training sessions, but he still occasionally comes up empty at the moment of truth. That's when he calls into action the coping strategies he has relied on for years to smooth over the rough patches of social interaction. If he's talking to two people who know him but don't know each other, and he can only recall one of their names, he'll say to the mystery guest, "Why don't you introduce yourself to Henry?" If both names escape him, Charles explains, "I'll say, 'Why don't you say hello to each other?' I try to say it in as offhand a way as possible."

In a one-on-one situation with someone vaguely familiar, he's an equally take-charge guy, simply going up to the person, shaking hands and graciously introducing himself. "The other person usually responds by saying, 'Oh, I'm so-and-so.' " But with alarming frequency, Charles says, "a little problem" develops when "the other person says, 'Nice to see you again.' And I think: *Who is that?* Then I back away and ask somebody who it is."

# Try the "Honey, I Shrunk My Memory" Solution

Among the CEOs and other top executives I've spoken with, one of the most popular tactics for solving the "I forgot" problem is relying on the spouse to run interference and extract the vital information from whatshisname. Here are a few samples of what I heard:

- "In social settings, if we meet someone I know, and I don't immediately introduce him to my wife by name, then she knows I don't remember and need help. Even though as a matter of etiquette I *should* be introducing her, she will introduce herself immediately, using her name. We've found that to be very effective."—Doug Braunstein, Head of Mergers and Acquisitions, J.P. Morgan investment bank
- "We have a secret arrangement. If I don't introduce her within thirty seconds, she will jump in and say, 'Hi, I'm Art's wife, Pat,' whereupon the name will come out. Always helpful."—Arthur F. Ryan, Chairman and CEO, Prudential Financial Inc.
- "I always warn my wife when we're a social pair: 'If I don't introduce you, it's because I don't remember their name. Please help me out and introduce yourself, and then we'll get their name again.' " —Mike Zisman, Executive Vice President for Strategy of Lotus Development Corp., a wholly owned subsidiary of IBM
- "We help each other, we have a sense of when either one doesn't remember a name. She knows to do that and I know to do that." —Dick Beatty, Chairman of the New York-based law firm Simpson, Thacher, Bartlett

# Let Them Sort It Out

Tom Quick, president of the financial services company Quick & Reilly, is renowned within the company for knowing the names of hundreds, if not thousands, of employees—right down to the messengers and mail room staff. But even he has the occasional panicked moment when someone familiar is bearing down on him at a business or social gathering and his memory flashes the "Out of Order" sign.

"I'll be talking with people when we're suddenly interrupted by another couple that walks up and I forget who they are," Tom tells me. "I say, 'Oh, I want you to meet my friends.' So I'll have the couple I've been talking to introduce themselves to this new couple, and I just step out. I have done that on more than one occasion. I feel that's a great way of not putting myself in an embarrassing situation."

# Use the Bait-and-Switch Technique

If you're face to face with someone who has no doubt told you his or her name but who's only an acquaintance, you can get away with this one. Just say, "I'm sorry, please tell me your name again." If they reply with their last name, say, "Oh, I know that. I meant, what's your first name?" If they reply with their first name, then: "Of course I know that. I meant, what's your last name?" Either way, you can feign a certain degree of familiarity—however lamely—while still getting the information you need.

# For Those with a Little Jerry Seinfeld in Them

You've got to have great timing for this one, but I've seen it get a big laugh—and get the information at the same time.

You: "I'm sorry, I've forgotten your last name. . . ."

Them: "Smith."

You, immediately: ". . . and your first name."

Ba-dum-dum.

# Throw a Hail Mary Pass

A variant of the bait-and-switch technique is just to say, "Would you please spell your name for me?" If they say "B-i-l-l- S-m-i-t-h" and stand there glaring, the only thing you can do is admit, "You caught me." The Hail Mary is best used if you have at least a faint thread of memory telling you the person has a slightly unusual name.

# Realize That Two Out of Three *Is* Bad

Paul Allaire, chairman and CEO of the Xerox Corp., tells me that he often loses names. "But I have something to cover that up," he says. "If I see three people and I know two and know I should know the third, then I won't use the name of any of the three so it's not obvious that I don't know Maria by name: 'Hello, Bob. Hello, Joe. Hello, what's-your-name.' It's better to do a hello, what's your name, what's your name, what's your name than it is to single one out."

# Let Your Body Language Say It All

When words (and memory) fail J. P. Morgan's Doug Braunstein, he compensates by becoming physically demonstrative. "I use physical touch as my crutch," Doug tells me. "To the extent that I don't remember someone's name, and I realize I should remember their name, I will put an arm around their shoulder or grasp a shoulder or an arm, or do some physical form of contact that tries to connect me to that individual. This is obviously within the context of appropriateness. But if you don't remember someone's name and you should, it's not a very positive reflection of their importance to you. A way to cover that is with a different form of intimacy as a connection."

# Use the Hubert H. Humphrey Memorial Lower-Lumbar Maneuver

Long before Dick Beatty became chairman of the white-shoe law firm Simpson, Thacher, Bartlett, he served as general counsel to the Department of Health, Education and Welfare in the Carter administration. A good friend in those days was former Vice President Hubert Humphrey, who was renowned for his ebullient spirit and warm rapport with supporters and fellow politicians.

One night Dick and Hubert were talking together at a social function in Washington when a third man greeted them both by name. Humphrey welcomed him into their conversation, and asked him with a look of concern, "How's your back?" The man replied his back was better and thanked Humphrey for his concern, adding, "It's amazing you even remember I had a bad back."

As the man walked away, Beatty turned to the former vice president and asked, "Who was that?"

"I'm afraid I have no idea," said Humphrey.

"But you even asked about his bad back."

*"Everybody* my age has a bad back," Humphrey replied. "Whenever I forget someone's name, I ask about their back."

# Go Fishing

Yes, you're stumped at the moment by the sort-of-familiar face in front of you, but maybe a little additional information will make everything fall into place. "It's been too long. When was the last time we saw each other?" Putting the face in context for your memory can elicit the name that goes with it. If it still doesn't come in . . .

# Take a Detour

One strategy is just to refuse to play Name That Name and call everyone something friendly but vague: "Champ," or "Professor," or "Captain." It used to be all right to call women "Dear," but these days that can land you on the politically incorrect list.

Dick Beatty mentions another politician with a tactic that falls under this heading. Former New York City mayor David Dinkins has what Beatty calls, not surprisingly, The David Dinkins Method: "He never uses anybody's name," Dick says. "It's always, 'Hey, buddy, how are you?' Everybody's 'buddy.' He carries pictures of *my* grandkids in his wallet because he really likes them, but he doesn't say, 'Hey, Dick, how are you?' It's 'Hey, buddy, how are you doing?' That method has worked very well for him." As for Dick himself, introducing someone he's just met to a third party can be one of the rare occasions when he finds himself in a tight spot. In that case, he says, kill 'em with kindness: "I say, 'This is one of the best lawyers in the country.' The other person will invariably introduce himself.'"

# Play a Card Game

Here's a trick a friend described to me but I never would have dreamt up. My friend had a coworker who always carried a few blank Rolodex cards and a pen in his jacket pocket. Whenever he saw a familiar face at a business event and sensed that he'd be unable to remember the name in time, he pulled out a blank card and smiled with great relief as his acquaintance approached. "Thank heaven you're here. We reconfigured the office and my Rolodex was misplaced when they moved things around. Could you write down your information?"

# Honesty Is the Best Policy, I

"Of course I remember you, but your *name* has slipped my mind." Mention whatever information you *do* remember about them—"We met last year at John and Alice's party"—just to show them that they're not a complete stranger.

# Honesty Is the Best Policy, II

"I'm sorry, I've just gone completely blank."

# Honesty Is the Best Policy, III

In the end, the only surefire option when you forget a name is George Walther's from *Power Talking: 50 Ways to Say What You Mean and Get What You Want*. Simply say: "Please remind me of your name." That's it. Don't explain, don't complain. Don't make any jokey excuses ("Since I turned fifty I don't remember anything," or "Since I had kids, I never get enough sleep," or "All I retain is water"). Say nothing defeatist. Don't tell yourself or anyone else that you have a bad memory, *because you don't have a bad memory*. You've only suffered a glitch in your memory training. The polite, executive-in-control thing to say is: "Please remind me of your name."

If the other person greets you by name and says, "Great to see you again," but you're drawing a blank, just say, "Please remind me of your name."

Or beat them to the punch: Introduce yourself and say, "Please remind me of your name."

The flip side of this is never allow someone you run into to struggle with recalling *your* name. Never say, "Remember me?" Unless, of course, you want to be remembered as a jerk. Instead, hit them with all the information they need to place you: "Hi, I'm Joe Smith. The last time we met was at the Chase Banking Forum in Tucson." In other words, *be your own host*.

# CHAPTER 15

# Memory That Lasts and Lasts

You only need to remember some names for an hour or two. Others for a week. Then there are the ones you know you'll need for years. I've saved the best for last. Maybe you've met one of my CEO clients who's impressed you. His secret? Read on. . . .

"Part of my concern about names and business contacts is that I know how *I* feel when somebody I've met before doesn't know my name. It's like saying, 'I didn't bother—you must have had so little consequence in what you were saying or what you were doing, I don't even remember who you are.' "

—*Steven Gluckstern, CEO of Zurich Global Asset Management*

The neuron strings that form the tendrils of a memory in your brain have one unfortunate characteristic: they begin withering away when neglected. Not always, and not entirely. We've all astonished ourselves by dredging up some utterly forgettable relic of information from the past—the Best Cinematography Academy Award winner from 1967 *(Bonnie and Clyde)* or your brother's third-grade teacher's name or who founded the Federal Reserve (Woodrow Wilson). But for the most part the general rule with memory-formation is harsh and unforgiving. No matter how vivid and accessible a new memory might be, the longer it goes unused, the weaker and sparser become the neuron strings that make it retrievable.

Obviously, memories of personal, emotional importance stay active longer and are more easily recalled. Seeing the birth of your child creates enough neuron strings to weave a neuron *rope*. But less vital matters—no matter how much importance you might try to attach to them intellectually—inevitably slip away if you let them gather dust.

The techniques you've learned in this book will certainly give you more power to remember names and faces than you've ever had before. FACE will get you all the way through those dinner affairs, business cocktails, convention get-togethers and other events where new names are pouring in your ear one after another—and in the past would have been just as quickly exiting out the other ear. The names and faces you "get" with FACE will remain with you for the short term—the day of the event and into the next. By using the NAME technique, you can lock down the information more securely in your memory. NAME can keep a new name alive for weeks, months or even years. But to make sure the name remains a strong, readily accessible presence, you'll need to make an effort to revisit the name occasionally in order to freshen up those neuron strings.

I have a memory client who declared war on the erosion of names and faces that he has worked hard to commit to his memory. Whenever a visitor comes to his office for the first time, Bill has a little ritual at the conclusion of the meeting. He steps outside his office with the visitor and asks his assistant to take a snapshot of the two of them smiling for the camera. The visitor is almost always flattered—Bill's memorializing this historic summit!—but the truth is that Bill actually doesn't care about having his own photograph taken with the visitor. He just wants to obtain an image of the person, and it would be too awkward to say, "Thanks for coming by. Oh, and please see my assistant so she can take your mug shot."

On the backs of the photographs, he records the person's name, a brief description of what was discussed in the meeting, and a few pieces of personal information (the names of the visitor's wife and kids, his favorite sports team, where he went to college—that sort of thing). Bill keeps the photos handy in a leather-bound box on his desk, and makes a habit of reviewing them while he's on the phone or just taking a break.

He's developing into something of a legend in his business for his "people skills," even though he originally sought help from me to improve what we both agree was an untrained, undistinguished memory and then started using his photo strategy to consolidate the progress he had made in working with me.

While not all of us have our own personal photographers to record the new people we meet, that doesn't mean we can't develop a long-term memory for names and faces.

# Make Names Your Own Little Obsession

Throughout this book, I've stressed the benefits of turning names into a sort of personal hobby. It's a hobby that can pay off. Being attentive to names, becoming curious about their origins, asking other people for details about how they got theirs—those are all elements of the ASK and COMMENT stages of FACE. The more you pursue your curiosity about names, the more natural it will seem, and the more comfortable you'll be talking with people about their names. And the more benefits you'll reap from FACE.

An extension of this approach to names is *using* them much more than you ever have before. *Become a user of names.* Speak out the names of friends, family, acquaintances, co-workers—everyone you see on a regular basis, but whose names you might not actually use all that often. Every time you say someone's name aloud, it sends a little jolt through your memory system that revitalizes your ability to recall that particular name.

Doing this builds up your repertoire of names for cross-referencing. By saying "Hi, Neil" to my neighbor, I've turned him into my prototypical "Neil." He's a much better connection for me than some vague memory of Neil Sedaka. In the future, every Neil I meet can be tied to next-door Neil. Which in turn makes my neighbor Neil even more deeply embedded in my memory.

Too many people make the mistake of taking for granted the names of the people they see every day—the security guard in the lobby of the building where you work, the handful of coworkers closest to your office or cubicle, people who live in your neighborhood whom you see all the time but don't socialize with very much. We give these folks a wave almost on a daily basis, maybe say, "Hey, how are you?" but we don't worry about remembering their names because, well, jeez, *we see them every day.* But then comes that moment when we suddenly need to remember their names and draw a complete blank. Your spouse drops by the office and you start to introduce him or her to your coworkers, only to turn to a person who's worked twenty feet away from you for the past year and say, "Honey, I'd like you to meet . . ."

Nothing! Not a syllable! Someone you may have spent more time with over the past year than your own children—and you can't remember his name! How could that be? Easy. You've probably spoken his name out loud fewer than half a dozen times. Sure, he's Don. Good old Don. Down-the-hall-Don. But when you actually see Don in the hall, or walk by his desk, or run into him in the copy room, the unforgettable Don only gets a "What's up?" or "How's it going?" And with each passing day, a little more of your memory-access for Don shuts down. If you had only said "How's it going, Don?" periodically over the course of the past twelve months, you and your spouse wouldn't be standing in the hallway with everyone staring expectantly while you want to crawl under your desk.

# Change the Context, Keep the Name

Here's a worse scenario. You go to introduce your spouse to your office mates and forget your *spouse's* name. Aaaiiieeee! You'll pay for that one. But it's not farfetched. I've seen it happen. It's an understandable goof. You're not accustomed to seeing this person, no matter how beloved they are, *at your office.* The usual domestic context is gone—the context that is heavily imprinted on your memory with spousal connotations—and instead you're confronted with this very familiar human being suddenly plunked down in surroundings that have zero spousal connotations.

That's easily cured. In addition to becoming a user of names, try to use your imagination to whisk people away from the context in which you're familiar with them and deposit them somewhere else. After meeting someone many times, I'll occasionally use some downtime to mentally dress them up in a tuxedo and send them out to a nightclub, or plunk them on the beach in the latest swimwear. Doesn't matter if they're the postman or a new client whose name I'm certain I'll want to hang on to for a long time. Seeing them in an alternative context—new clothes, new job!—burns a fresh path into the memory. And that makes it much harder for access to be denied when you're standing in the shopping mall and are suddenly confronted by a smiling, terribly familiar face waiting to be acknowledged (Is he the plumber? The guy from accounting? Uncle Nick?).

These recommendations apply both to your life at home and work. It's all part of giving *names themselves* a more prominent role in the life of your mind. Prominence doesn't mean preoccupation: it's not a big commitment of time. Taking the trouble to use the names of others in passing conversations, entertaining yourself with an imaginary glimpse of them in new clothes and settings—shouldn't take more than a second or two. But the benefits are enormous and long-lasting.

# Photo Finish

I realize that not every name and face you want to remember comes your way on a regular basis and presents itself for a memory-refresher course. This is particularly true in business, when you might see someone from one of your company's distant offices at a conference once or twice a year and maybe in your own offices occasionally. Or maybe your company's so big that there are other employees elsewhere on your floor whose names you need to remember but whom you only see once in a blue moon.

That's where a corporate face book comes in awfully handy. Many companies maintain books that are essentially photographic rosters of their employees. The books usually sit around gathering dust, perhaps getting a quick once-over from bored visitors waiting out by the front desk. *These books are gold!* You might be the only person in the company who anyone has ever seen *studying* the face book, but do yourself a favor and review it once in a while. Practice NAME on the photos of people you want to remember. Maybe even write down a MORPH for the names next to the pictures and then ENTWINE it while looking at them.

If your company doesn't have a face book, consider dropping a hint to the office manager (or whoever handles that sort of thing for your company) about having seen an impressive face book at another company's offices. Suggest that it might be a nice little morale booster if your outfit had one, too. One client of mine has had the face book put on his computer as a screen-saver. He can bring it up by division, by floor, by first or last name—you name it. He also had a Human Resources person take photos of people at their desks, so that he could see, for instance, Fred's assistant, Ilene, in the location where he would usually encounter her.

*Every* office has someone who's a keeper of the Party Pictures—those snapshots that everyone got a big laugh out of when they came back from the December holidays and then promptly forgot about. The next time there's a party, borrow the photos soon afterward, make color photocopies of them and identify as many people as you can, even the spouses, by writing the names down in the white space around the pictures. If you can't ID them all, find out who they are—get your secretary or assistant to help out.

Review the photos immediately before the next office party, and put in a request for a set of prints when the next batch of photos comes out. You might not need to know the names of everyone in the photographs on a long-term basis, but the exercise heightens your name awareness. For the names that you're sure you need to know long-term, use the NAME technique, just as you did with the face book.

What if people discover that you're going to such lengths to remember the names of everyone in the office? Won't they be disappointed, suspecting that you care so little about them that you have to work at remembering their names? Far from it. If anything, they'll come away even more impressed that you're willing to devote so much time and energy to remembering names. They might even wonder if they shouldn't be doing more on that score themselves.

# Thank You, PDA!

One of the great boons of the technological revolution—at least in my view—is the emergence of digital photography and the ability to take photos and display them almost anywhere. There's a wristwatch that would make James Bond suffer gadget-envy with its ability to snap photos, display them on the watch face and transfer them to a PC. Personal Digital Assistants like the Sony CLIÉ can display photographs of faces in its address book—a great breakthrough in the never-ending battle to attach names to faces.

I suspect that it won't be too long before it's not at all unusual for two business people who've just met to go through the following process. Instead of exchanging business cards, they'll whip out their PDAs, snap photos of each other and log in any pertinent information. Of course, it might lead to a new version of what I call the Name Badge Effect, where people assume they know a name because it's right there in front of them, without making an effort to bind it to their memory. We'll be creating digital archives of every significant business contact we've ever had, with the ability to review their names and faces whenever we like. With that sort of material readily accessible, and by applying the NAME technique to every name/face you review, you'll be able to develop long-term memory for the information that will last until well after you've retired! (If you're sitting at poolside in St. Bart's thirty years from now, remembering Sid, the guy you met at a conference in Detroit in 2003, you have my permission to hit the Delete button.)

But until the photo-capable PDA is ubiquitous, I recommend an old-school way of keeping track of the new people you meet in the course of your business life. In your daily appointment book or electronic organizer, jot down a quick reminder about the significant people you met that day. Don't wait a day or two. *Be aware that most memory loss happens in the first twenty-four hours.* Record the name, a couple of physical traits (tall guy, brown hair), notes on a previous conversation and where his office is in relation to the front desk. Those jottings should help you to focus on who he is and what he looks like. At the end of the week, review the information you've recorded and try to conjure up the faces of all the people you made notations about.

You'll lose some of the name-face connections, but even if you remember fifty percent, it will be better than nothing. At the end of the next week, review that week and the week before. Then move on, starting fresh the following week with more names and faces. At the end of the fourth week, go back and review the entire month. Start over again with the next month, using the same process, and then at the end, do a review of both. Then start the sixty-day process over again. If keeping these records in your appointment book feels too much like work, make the notations on the backs of business cards you receive, and dedicate a place somewhere on your desk or in it where you can keep the cards and refer back to them.

# The Clintonian Approach

I know that some of you out there may have been silently griping as you read this that it all seems *too* much like work. I agree. But what we're talking about here is supercharging your ability to remember names and faces for the long term, specifically because it can reward you with so many career benefits.

*Remembering names and faces is the greatest skill you never learned.*

It will enhance your career opportunities—shouldn't it require a bit of work to achieve?

Consider this: For most of his adult life before he was elected president, Bill Clinton made it a habit to take a few minutes before going to bed at night to jot down notes on every contact he made that day. These weren't just a few scribbles on a cocktail napkin; Clinton entered the data on 3x5 index cards just as his hero JFK did, recording the name, time and place of the meeting and any other relevant information. Over the years, Clinton amassed a collection of cards the *New York Times* estimated at 10,000, which he would regularly review to keep the memories fresh in his mind. One of the traits that made Clinton among the most adept politicians of the past half-century was his legendary ability to remember names. As I discussed in Chapter 3, "Why It Matters," Clinton's name-recall skills have awed countless people over the years, people who had no reason to expect him to remember their names. So has his ability to focus on individuals and make them feel singled out for his attention.

"I have never seen a more effective one-on-one communicator in a large group than President Clinton," Art Ryan, chairman and CEO of Prudential Financial Inc., tells me. "He is extraordinary. He could be in a room with three hundred people, and when he was talking to you, you honestly believed there was no one else in the room. One of the most effective people I have ever seen in my life, in terms of just being able to take that forty-five seconds, minute and a half, two minutes—it can appear much longer, but generally it is not—and totally engage himself."

Of course, Clinton's technique is about connecting with people and inspiring them, but something else is going on as well. He is drinking in information about the person he's meeting, information that he knows he'll be needing later, and likely recording on an index card. If a camera crew followed Clinton through a reception, you might see him employing—without necessarily realizing it—the basic elements that make up FACE, over and over again.

The take-away here is that you can't receive a piece of information once and expect to remember it long-term. (How much high-school algebra do you remember?) The information has to be reinforced, and in order to do that you need to come up with a strategy for doing so. I've laid out some suggestions here for achieving long-term retention, but other ideas may occur to you. By all means put them to use. I hope that you'll make the effort to preserve the benefits of using the FACE and NAME techniques, because mastering the skill of remembering names and faces can change your life.

Does that sound like a reach? I don't think so. More than a dozen heads of large corporations I spoke with for this book have attested to the importance of remembering names and faces as a business skill. But in addition to being a useful career tool, remembering names and faces by using the FACE and NAME techniques allows you to approach business and social interactions with a confidence that few people naturally possess. You're not walking into a dinner party, reception, or a conference with the vague hope that you'll make a good impression on the people you meet. You're not relying solely on whatever social skills you may have haphazardly developed over the years. The FACE and NAME techniques allow you to enter any room, no matter how full of strangers, with an *achievable* agenda. They also show you the way to take control of a conversation and steer it toward a goal—getting a fix on the name and face of every new person you meet. What's more, you'll be making the encounter as pleasant as possible for the other person. Remember, the sound of your name is music to your ears.

There are efficient, practical ways to ensure your long-term retention of names and faces.
- Use the names of everyone you see regularly. No more "Hiya!"
- Imagine familiar folks in unfamiliar clothing and settings.
- Become a note-taker, whether on your Palm Pilot or in your daily appointment book. Who'd you meet? Where? When? What did they look like? Then regularly review the information. If you can, cross-reference by city, company, division, floor, title.
- Create name file cards with MORPH included.
- Photos are a godsend. Office-party pictures, the corporate face book, whatever. Practice the NAME technique on them!
- Check out new technology for PDAs and other devices that can become your photo and info archives.

Sweat the details. A little work at long-term retention will have long-lasting career benefits.

# CHAPTER 16

# Closing the Deal

Now you've got all my trade secrets
for remembering names and faces.
Certainly, these skills can have the same
beneficial effects on your career
that they've had on mine!

"Remembering names and faces is absolutely priceless in the business world. It makes people feel good about themselves and about you."

—*Paul Allaire, Chairman and CEO of Xerox Corp.*

At the beginning of this book, I remarked on the irrationality of the common lament, "I have a terrible memory for names." That kind of thinking is akin to complaining about what an awful skier you are when you've never had a skiing lesson in your life. I volunteered to be your mental ski instructor, sharing techniques that enable you to capitalize on your natural—but underutilized and untrained—memory power.

Start out on little hills first, using just the FACE technique in one-on-one situations where not too much is at stake. Nobody goes straight from the first ski lesson to a near-vertical black-diamond mogul field. Build your confidence in casual encounters and low-stress settings.

If you currently remember one or two names of people you meet at a dinner, use FACE with the goal of remembering three. Once you've done that, add another one to your goal. Don't attempt to use FACE or NAME in an important situation until you feel comfortable with the techniques. *In fact, don't use NAME until FACE is almost a reflex—until it has basically altered the way you approach meeting strangers.*

For many readers, if not the vast majority, mastering the FACE technique will have such a transformative effect on the way they interact with people and on their ability to remember names and faces that they may never even feel the need to step up and put NAME into action. I've worked so long using both FACE and NAME in tandem that I don't even consciously think about it. Deploying FOCUS, ASK, COMMENT and EMPLOY, as well as NOMINATE, ARTICULATE, MORPH and ENTWINE has become second nature to me. Then again, remembering names and faces is vital to my career. I've put these approaches to almost constant use for years.

When I'm performing in a room of 100 people, I may have to nominate 20 noses, 20 head shapes and 20 eye regions. There might be eight people named John. But the techniques still work. The individual name is connected to the individual face, and each face *tells* me its name. I review the information I've gathered after I've spoken with a few groups of people, and if I find that I've momentarily lost a John or a Mike or a Susan, I'll strengthen the ENTWININGS of their MORPHS. I may realize that I need to add more elements from A NOVEL COLOR PICTURE—usually more color or emotion. Sometimes I even switch MORPHS if the one I've chosen isn't working. If one night it seems I'm losing Johns, maybe I'll switch to long-johns as the MORPH, utilizing the "N" for "new" in NOVEL by creating a fresh image. If microphones lose their vividness for me, I might switch to oars (think "Michael Row Your Boat Ashore").

Some nights I feel like a highly trained athlete who's "in the zone." Maybe with a quarter of the people, I'll need to see the face and use my techniques to remember their names. But three-quarters of the people have names that just seem to jump out at me. She just *is* Frieda. He simply *is* Stan. I'm cross-referencing by age, by people I know. In my mind, their face merges with others in their name file. The connections are so strong that I don't even need a reminder. But unless I know that I'm going to need the information again, it's going to be gone within a few days.

And then there's sex and greed, two of my greatest strengths—when it comes to remembering names, that is. I don't even have to FOCUS consciously in two very specific situations if I'm using FACE: when I'm meeting an attractive woman, and when I'm meeting a potential client. I'm a very happily married man, but it's a fact of life: the names of attractive women I meet just stick in my mind for weeks or months after I meet them. And I guess that since my entrepreneurial tendencies have been switched on since I was about ten years old, I have a keenly developed sense of where new business lies. Put me in a room with thirty potential clients and it's a done deal—I've got all their names, no problem.

My memory has become so adept that it does many of the steps of FACE and NAME on its own. But I fall down if I take it for granted. For instance, if I say, "Oh, yes, Jeff, like my brother." That may fly in a small group, but it's fatal when I'm working with dozens of people. There was an event I once did for 150 people in which one man had a name I simply could not remember. As it turned out, his name was Benjamin. I took it so much for granted that it went in one ear and out the other.

*I didn't remember it because, without my techniques, my memory is only average. People think I have a rare gift, but what I really have is a dedication to applying myself to remembering names and faces. I know how important that skill can be.*

Actually using the FACE and NAME techniques, putting them into action over and over again, is crucial to maximizing their benefits. Over time, you'll find that the two start to merge into each other. By now, I certainly don't need to consciously use FOCUS and ASK—they happen automatically. I know what I'm there for: I have to get the name clearly. My conscious FOCUS is instead on a feature, almost before the conversation has begun. I've become so good at MORPHING that almost as the name comes in, it goes through a MORPH filter. While I'm EMPLOYING the name in conversation, I'm simultaneously ENTWINING it. Once you become adept at putting them to use, the two techniques become one.

I hope you haven't just read this book from beginning to end thinking that maybe some of the ideas will percolate in your mind and instantly improve your ability to remember names and faces. It doesn't work that way. Which is why I urged you to go out and try FACE in real-world sit-

**CLOSING THE DEAL**

uations before moving on. Many memory-improvement books have been written over the years that presuppose little need for practice. As a result, the books weren't very useful and ultimately left readers feeling skeptical of the idea that their memory power could really be enhanced.

# Benefits Package

There have also been many books written over the years to answer the question: How can I get people to like me? On the surface, that's not what this book is about, but it's certainly one of the benefits of developing your power to remember names and faces. Making it clear that someone you've just met is unforgettable to you is perhaps the most attractive kind of flattery ever invented. It makes the other person feel great about him or her and feel warmly toward you. Yet you haven't done anything other than achieve what we all aspire to: a good memory for names. You haven't cooked up a bogus compliment or shown transparently false enthusiasm in an effort to butter up the other person. You've performed the simple-yet-rarely-witnessed feat of not forgetting the name of this stranger you just met.

But the social benefits are greater than that. Think about the steps of FACE. They're practically a how-to guide for improving your self-confidence and your "likability" factor:

- FOCUS requires you to truly concentrate your attention on the person across from you. The message you're sending is that at this moment in time, nothing else in the world is as fascinating as the conversation you're having. Who wouldn't like to be on the receiving end of that message?
- ASK allows you to make it clear exactly how interested you are in the other person. You're saying: "You're so important to me that I want to make sure I've got every detail about you correctly."
- COMMENT does two things. It tells the other person: "No, you weren't just imagining how fascinated I am by you. I've assimilated what you've told me, and already feel so at ease with the information that I'm happy to talk about it." COMMENT also gives you a chance

to show the other person that you're pleasant, smart and, perhaps, even funny.

- EMPLOY is the cherry on top of this lovely dessert you're serving up. It says: "You're so memorable and have already become such a familiar presence in my mind that I feel completely comfortable using your name in conversation."

# From Dreading to Ready

The list above addresses the effect that using FACE has on the recipient. A wonderful side benefit of the technique is the way it can transform the way you perform in social situations. In many, many among us, the prospect of meeting strangers at a cocktail party or in a conference room can induce a feeling of complete dread. What will I talk about? What if I don't know anyone? What if I don't have anything to say? With thoughts like that, no wonder so many folks greet the prospect of going into a roomful of strangers like they were being led to the gallows. And no wonder those negative expectations often turn out to be self-fulfilling prophecies. The FACE technique is a tool that allows you to enter any room, filled with any number of unfamiliar faces, confident that you will have something to talk about with anyone you encounter.

Isn't that terrific? I wish I had known about this stuff when I was a teenager; my social life would have been a lot happier. I'm certainly glad I discovered it as an adult. Training my natural memory to become a powerful tool for remembering names and faces changed my life and my career. I've been performing magic since I was a boy, but magic tricks tend to have a distancing effect between the performer and the audience. I'm on the inside and know the secret, you're on the outside and can't figure it out. It wasn't until I began demonstrating my ability to remember names and faces that my career went into high gear. Suddenly, I was connecting with audiences in a way that, my clients tell me, rarely happens in the entertainment world. I was on a first-name basis with them! The sense of goodwill that generates is enormous. So does the sense of astonishment in the audience when I pull off the "trick."

# The Ultimate Win-Win

Magic performances are all about making a series of miracles happen and getting a gratifying response of pure wonder in return. But no miracle I perform has ever gotten the reaction that I get when I remember the names of 100 people in an audience, and certainly no audience response I've ever felt comes close to the pure pleasure people take in being recognized at a moment when they never expected it.

You'll feel that way too—when you use the FACE and NAME techniques, and are able to greet someone you barely know by name. There's nothing quite like seeing the other person light up when he says, "I can't believe you remembered my name!" Those words are golden, because you've not only made the other person happy at that moment, but in doing so you've made yourself exceptionally memorable as well. It's a classic win-win.

Don't you forget it!

# America's Top 40

I've done the research for you:
I studied the most popular names in past
decades and compiled a list of the 40 men's
and 40 women's names you're most likely
to encounter in the business world today.
Plus: how to adapt the names for use with the
FACE and NAME techniques.

It was all very well for me to explain the NAME technique in Chapter 7. And it was fine for me to tell you in Chapter 11 how to MORPH a nondescript name like Bill into a vivid visual substitute like a duck's snapping bill or a stunningly expensive dry-cleaning bill that's so long it unfurls like a roll of toilet paper. But there are many, many names out there that you're likely to run into on a regular basis and I don't want you to have to scramble every time to dream up your own MORPHS for them.

I've gone back through lists and lists of popular names through the years and assembled what I believe is a definitive list of the 80 names—40 for men, 40 for women—that are currently the most frequently occurring names for people between ages 25 and 60. In other words, most of the business people you'll be meeting and whose names you'll want to remember. Those names are on the left-hand side of the table that begins on page 216. To give you a place to start, the 20 most popular names are printed in red.

In the middle column, you'll find my suggestions for well-known people you might want to keep in mind for use during the COM-

MENT stage of FACE so you can cross-reference new names with ones that your memory has already taken on-board.

*But far better would be names that have some personal connection to you: your Uncle Alan, rather than Alan Greenspan, your sister Jane instead of Jane Fonda. An added emotional connection to a name, of a friend or family member, will make a name much more memorable in the FACE technique than if it simply has celebrity attached to it.*

The right-hand column contains the MORPHS I recommend for each name when you're employing the NAME technique. These are the MORPHS I use and have had great success with.

Don't feel you have to memorize this entire table. Familiarize yourself with it first, then really concentrate on the top ten names, printed in red. Once you've got them down, try another ten, and so on. If that feels too much like homework, just review the table from time to time—you'll commit more of it to memory than you realize, and at the very least it will plant the seeds of new ways of thinking about names.

| TOP 40 MEN'S NAMES | | |
|---|---|---|
| Name | For the *FACE* Technique: That Reminds Me of . . . | For the *NAME* Technique: MORPH |
| Alan, Allen, Al | The Fed's Alan Greenspan, actor Alan Alda, Allen Funt of *Candid Camera,* gangster Al Capone | Alien, a lion, owl |
| Andrew, Andy | Andrew Carnegie, artist Andy Warhol, Andy Rooney of *60 Minutes,* comic Andy Kaufman | Android, anty (covered with ants) |
| **Bill** | Bill Gates, PBS host Bill Moyers, President Bill Clinton | Duck's bill |
| **Bob,** Robert | Sports Announcer Bob Costas, musician Bob Dylan; actors Robert Redford, Robert De Niro | Bobsled, bobcat, robber |
| Brian | Beach Boy Brian Wilson, actor Brian Dennehy, newscaster Brian Williams | Brain, brine, fryin' (pan) |
| Bruce | Batman alter ego Bruce Wayne, musician Bruce Springsteen, actor Bruce Willis | Bruise, bruiser |

| Name | For the *FACE* Technique: That Reminds Me of . . . | For the *NAME* Technique: MORPH |
|---|---|---|
| Charles | Charles de Gaulle, Charles Lindbergh, talk-show host Charlie Rose, actor Charlie Sheen, Charles Manson | Chars (charcoals), chairs |
| Chris, Christopher | Comedian Chris Rock, Christopher Columbus, actor Christopher Reeve | Christmas tree, kiss |
| Dan, Daniel | Actor Dan Aykroyd, Daniel Boone, Daniel Webster | Dam, Dance |
| **Dave,** David | Columnist Dave Barry, talk-show host David Letterman | Dive (diving board), divot, shave |
| Dennis | Actors Dennis Quaid, Dennis Weaver; Dennis the Menace | Tennis, dentist |
| Don, Donald | Donald Trump, Don Juan, baseball pitcher Don Larsen, Don Corleone (*The God-father*) | Donut |
| Doug, Douglas | General Douglas MacArthur, actor Douglas Fairbanks Jr., "Doug" (children's TV show) | Dugout canoe, shovel (dug) |
| Ed, Edward | Actor Ed Asner, former New York City mayor Ed Koch, journalist Edward R. Murrow | Bed, horse ("Mr. Ed") |
| Frank | Frank Sinatra, musician Frank Zappa, sports broadcaster Frank Gifford | Frankfurter |
| Gary | Actor Gary Cooper, comedian Gary Shandling, golfer Gary Player | Garage |
| George | President George W. Bush, actor George Clooney, boxer George Foreman, George Washington | Gorge, powdered wig (George Washington) |
| Greg, Gregory | Actors Gregory Peck, Greg Kinnear; performer Gregory Hines, golfer Greg Norman | Grog (tankard of ale) |
| Jack | Golfer Jack Nicklaus, boxer Jack Dempsey, actor Jack Nicholson | Car jack, jack-in-the-box, jack o' lantern |

| Name | For the _FACE_ Technique: That Reminds Me of . . . | For the _NAME_ Technique: MORPH |
|---|---|---|
| Jeff, Jeffrey | Actor Jeff Bridges, producer Jeffrey Katzenberg, comedian Jeff Foxworthy | Jif (peanut butter), chef |
| Jerry | Comedian Jerry Seinfeld, musician Jerry Lee Lewis, religious leader Jerry Falwell | Cherry |
| **Jim, James** | Actors Jim Carrey, James Earl Jones; TV newsman Jim Lehrer, President James Madison, James Bond | Jungle gym, Slim Jim, chains |
| Joe, Joseph | G. I. Joe, baseball manager Joe Torre, Joe DiMaggio, publisher Joseph Pulitzer, Joseph Stalin | Sloppy Joe, joe (coffee), show (curtains going up) |
| **John** | Musician John Lennon, actor John Wayne, John the Baptist, President John F. Kennedy, 20 Popes by that name | John (toilet) |
| Keith | Musician Keith Richards, actor Keith Carradine, musician Keith Moon | Keys |
| Ken, Kenneth | Baseball player Ken Griffey, Jr., writer Ken Kesey, actor Kenneth Branagh; Barbie's boyfriend, Ken | Can (metal garbage can) |
| Kevin | Actors Kevin Spacey, Kevin Costner, Kevin Bacon, Kevin Kline | Cave-in |
| **Mark** | Mark Twain, swimmer Mark Spitz, baseball player Mark McGwire, artist Mark Rothko | Marker |
| Matt, Matthew | Actors Matt Damon, Matthew Broderick; reporter Matt Drudge, writer Matthew Arnold | Doormat |
| **Mike,** Michael | Michael Jordan, singer Michael Jackson, actor Michael Caine; the song "Michael Row Your Boat Ashore"; this is the most common name in the Western world | Mike (microphone) |

216

| Name | For the FACE Technique: That Reminds Me of . . . | For the NAME Technique: MORPH |
|---|---|---|
| Neil | Astronaut Neil Armstrong, musician Neil Young, playwright Neil Simon | Nail |
| Paul | Musician Paul McCartney, actor Paul Newman, Paul Revere | Pail, pole |
| Phil, Phillip | Hockey player Phil Esposito, actor Phil Hartman, Senator Phil Gramm, poet Philip Larkin, writer Philip Roth | Fillet, gas-pump nozzle (fill 'er up) |
| **Rich,** Richard | Performer Rich Little, President Richard Nixon, composer Richard Wagner, politician Richard Gephardt | Rich-heart, riches (coins or treasure) |
| Ron, Ronald | President Ronald Reagan, director Ron Howard, musician Ron Wood | Run (a stocking), Ronald McDonald |
| Scott | Writer Scott Turow, composer Scott Joplin, basketball player Scottie Pippin | Scott towels, Scotch, bagpipes |
| **Steve,** Steven, Stephen | Actor Steve McQueen, football player Steve Young, producer-director Steven Spielberg, Apple founder Steve Jobs | Stove, sleeve |
| Tim | Actor Tim Allen, baseball broadcaster Tim McCarver, singer Tiny Tim | Timer |
| **Tom,** Thomas | Actor Tom Cruise, golfer Tom Watson, writer Tom Wolfe, President Thomas Jefferson, inventor Thomas A. Edison | Tommy gun, tom-tom |
| Tony | Singer Tony Bennett, inspirational speaker Tony Robbins, baseball player Tony Gwynn; actors Tony Curtis, Tony Danza | Tony Award, Tony the Tiger (Frosted Flakes cereal) |

## TOP 40 WOMEN'S NAMES

| Name | For the *FACE* Technique: That Reminds Me of . . . | For the *NAME* Technique: MORPH |
| --- | --- | --- |
| Amy | Actress Amy Irving, singer Amy Grant, writer Amy Tan; the song "Once in Love with Amy" | Target (*aiming* at one) |
| Angela, Angie | Actresses Angela Lansbury, Angie Dickinson; activist Angela Davis | Angel, jello |
| Ann, Anne, Annie | Columnist Ann Landers, politician Ann Richards, diarist Anne Frank, Annie Oakley | Ant, Raggedy Ann |
| **Barbara** | Former First Lady Barbara Bush, Barbra Streisand, TV journalist Barbara Walters | Barbed wire, barber, Barbie doll |
| Carol | Model Carol Alt; actresses Carol Burnett, Carol Channing, Carol Kane | Coral, caroler (Christmas singer) |
| **Cathy,** Catherine | Olympian Cathy Rigby, Catherine the Great, actress Catherine Zeta-Jones | Cat, cats run (cats running) |
| Cheryl | Model Cheryl Tiegs, actress Cheryl Ladd | Chair |
| Christine, Chris | Politician Christine Todd Whitman, tennis player Chris Evert | Christmas tree |
| **Deborah,** Debbie | Singer Deborah Harry, TV newscaster Deborah Norville, actress Debbie Reynolds | Debutante, deputy |
| Denise | Actress Denise Richards | Dead knees |
| Diane, Diana | Actresses Diane Keaton, Diana Rigg; TV journalist Diane Sawyer, singer Diana Ross | Dyein' (tie-dyed cloth) |
| Donna | Designer Donna Karan, singer Donna Summer | Donut, Donald Duck |
| Eileen | Modeling agency owner Eileen Ford, actress Eileen Brennan | An eye leaning, I-beam |
| Elizabeth, Liza, Beth, Betty | Actresses Elizabeth Shue, Elizabeth Taylor; singer Liza Minnelli, former First Lady Betty Ford, Queen Elizabeth | Lizard, lizard bath |

| Name | For the FACE Technique: That Reminds Me of . . . | For the NAME Technique: MORPH |
|---|---|---|
| Gail | Sprinter Gail Devers, writer Gail Sheehy | Gale, gill |
| Jane | Actress Jane Fonda, writer Jane Austen, scientist Jane Goodall | Chain |
| Janet | Singer Janet Jackson, former Attorney General Janet Reno | Jam, jammed net |
| Jennifer, Jenny | Tennis player Jennifer Capriati; actresses Jennifer Aniston, Jennifer Beals, Jenny McCarthy | Janitor, penny |
| Joan | Singers Joan Jett, Joan Baez; comedian Joan Rivers, writer Joan Didion | Phone, Joan of Arc (burning stake), Sloppy Joe |
| Judy | Singer Judy Garland, actress Judy Davis | Judo, Punch and Judy, ruby slippers (Judy Garland) |
| Julie | Jockey Julie Krone; actresses Julie Andrews, Julie Hagerty | Jewels |
| **Karen** | Singer Karen Carpenter, artist Karen Finley, actress Karen Black | Carrot, corn, carton |
| Kathleen, Kathy | Opera singer Kathleen Battle, actress Kathleen Turner, actress Kathy Bates | Cats, cats lean(ing), cat latrine |
| Kelly | Actresses Kelly LeBrock, Kelly Lynch, Kelly McGillis | Kelly girl, belly |
| **Kimberly**, Kim | Actresses Kim Novak, Kim Basinger, singer Kim Carnes | Kimono, timber |
| Laura, Lauren, Laurie | Actresses Laura Dern, Lauren Bacall; model Lauren Hutton, musician Laurie Anderson; the song "Laura" | Laurel, lard |
| **Linda** | TV journalist Linda Ellerbee, actress Linda Lavin, singer Linda Ronstadt | Lint |
| Lisa | Actress Lisa Kudrow, Lisa Marie Presley | Mona Lisa, lease a _____ |

| Name | For the FACE Technique: That Reminds Me of . . . | For the NAME Technique: MORPH |
|---|---|---|
| Margaret, Marge, Peggy | Former British Prime Minister Margaret Thatcher, anthropologist Margaret Mead, Marge Simpson, Miss Piggy | Market, margarine, barge, piggy |
| **Mary** | Actress Mary Tyler Moore, writer Mary Shelley, Mary Poppins, George M. Cohan's song "Mary" | Merry-go-round, Mary-had-a-little-lamb |
| Michelle | Figure skater Michelle Kwan, actress Michelle Pfeiffer | Microphone-in-a-shell, marshal, a bell (the Beatles' "Michelle, ma belle . . .") |
| **Nancy** | Former First Lady Nancy Reagan, writer Nancy Mitford, singer Nancy Wilson | Ants see (with glasses), nun |
| Nicole | Actress Nicole Kidman | Nickel |
| Pamela, Pam | Ambassador Pamela Harriman, actress Pamela Anderson, tennis player Pam Shriver | Pan |
| **Patricia** | Writer Patricia Highsmith, actress Patricia Neal, singer Pat Benatar | Pat of butter |
| Paula | TV journalist Paula Zahn, singer Paula Abdul | Pail, pole |
| Sandra | Performer Sandra Bernhard, actress Sandra Bullock, Supreme Court Justice Sandra Day O'Connor | Sand, sander |
| **Sharon** | Actress Sharon Stone | Share Iron (it has two handles) |
| Susan, Sue | Suffragist Susan B. Anthony, writer Susan Sontag, actress Susan Sarandon | Sioux, Lazy Susan, suit |
| Tracy | Singer Tracy Chapman, tennis player Tracy Austin, actress Tracy Pollan | Trace feet, trachea |

# ACKNOWLEDGMENTS

This book began in conversations with John Needham, Geoff Colvin and Eric Rayman.

Thanks to Gary Johnston and the members of the Stockbridge Sportsman's Club, Rose Brooks and everyone at Seagram's Spirits and Wines Group, Scott Paige and my friends at Mitsubishi and the Fasciani family. Shonna Valeska, for such great photos. Mario Carrandi, for the Ringlings and much more. Bob Elliott, for permission to use "Memory Expert."

Thanks to my preview readers for their pithy and brutal comments: Gene Anderson, Sy Levy, Chris Soth and Matt Walker.

Thanks to all the people who so generously gave their time for interviews, especially if their wittiest remarks didn't make the final draft:

Paul Allaire
Dennis Alter
Dick Beatty
Mike Bloomberg
Jim Borden
Doug Braunstein
Charles Bronfman
Tatiana Cooley
Ellen duBellay
Steven Gluckstern
John Huey
Bob Hurst
Dorothea Johnson
Dr. Eric Kandel
Philippe Krakowsky
Marie-Josée Kravis

Cynthia Lett
Joe Loose
Bob Marbut
Don Marron
Dr. James McGaugh
Dr. Fredric T. Perlman
Tom Quick
Joan Rappoport
Ben Rosen
Art Ryan
Marie Seymour
Jolene Sykes
Larry Tisch
Alex von Bidder
Brad Warner
Sandy Warner

Mike Zisman

This book is as much Mark Lasswell's as mine, and I thank him for the extraordinary amount of work he put into it.

"Benjamin's astounding memory, wit and personality are sure to make any high-level corporate event a success. When you add his incredible magic to the mix you have an unforgettable entertainment experience."
—Paul A. Allaire, Chairman and CEO, Xerox Corporation

"Benjamin's memory act is spectacular. His ability to remember the names of everyone in the audience, well over 150 people in each of four performances for Sprint, is unforgettable. His sleight-of-hand magic is equally amazing. But, even more extraordinary is his ability to charm and engage everyone in his performance and create the kind of warm, friendly atmosphere we strive for at Sprint Corporation events."
—William T. Esrey, Chairman and CEO, Sprint Corporation

"Benjamin is a stunningly understated performer . . . that is, he is sublimely captivating before you realize how grandly talented he is!"
—Gerald M. Levin, Chairman and CEO, Time Warner, Inc.

"The greatest act I've ever seen."
—Andy Rooney, author and *60 Minutes* correspondent